From the
Diakonia of Christ
to the Diakonia of
the Apostles

International Theological Commission
Historico-Theological Research Document

HillenbrandBooks

Chicago / Mundelein

North American Edition of FROM THE DIAKONIA OF CHRIST TO THE DIAKONIA OF THE APOSTLES © 2004 Archdiocese of Chicago: Liturgy Training Publications, 1800 North Hermitage Avenue, Chicago IL 60622-1101; 1-800-933-1800, fax 1-800-933-7094, e-mail orders@ltp.org. All rights reserved. See our website at *www.ltp.org.*

Hillenbrand Books is an imprint of Liturgy Training Publications (LTP) and The Liturgical Institute/University of St. Mary of the Lake. The Hillenbrand Series is focused on contemporary and classical theological thought concerning the Liturgy of the Catholic Church. Further information about **Hillenbrand Books** is available from LTP at *www.usml.edu/liturgicalinstitute;* 847-837-4542; University of the Lake/Mundelein Seminary, 1000 East Maple, Mundelein IL 60060.

Please note that this translation of the original French text was produced by the Catholic Truth Society at the behest of the International Theological Commission and has not been submitted to the Holy See for official *recognitio.*

Cover photo © The Crosiers Gene Plaisted, OCS.

Printed in the United States of America.

Library of Congress Cataloging-in-Publication Data 2004101488

ISBN 1-59525-000-X

HDIAK

Contents

Chapter 1

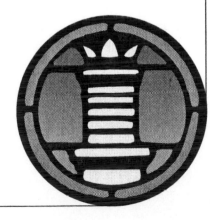

From the Diakonia of Christ to the Diakonia of the Apostles

I. DIAKONIA OF CHRIST AND CHRISTIAN EXISTENCE

Through the incarnation of the Word who is God and by whom all was made (cf. John 1:1–18) the strangest revolution imaginable has come about. The *Kyrios*, Lord, becomes the *diakonos*, servant, of all. The Lord God comes out to meet us in his Servant Jesus Christ, the only Son of God (Romans 1:3), who, being in the "form of God," "did not see in the form of God a prize to be coveted, but emptied himself, taking the form of a slave. Having become like men . . . he abased himself and became obedient to death, even death on a cross" (Philippians 2:6–8).

The essence of being a Christian can thus be grasped in a Christological perspective. Christian existence is a sharing in the *diakonia* or service which God himself fulfilled in favor of mankind; it likewise leads to an understanding of the fulfillment of mankind. Being a Christian means following Christ's example in putting oneself at the service of others to the point of self-renunciation and self-giving, for love.

Baptism confers this *diakonein*, power of service, on every Christian. Through it, by virtue of their participation in the *diakonia*, *leiturgia* and *martyria*, the service, worship and witness of the Church, Christians cooperate in Christ's own diakonia for the salvation of mankind. As members of the Body of Christ, all should become servants of one another, using the charisms which they have received for the building up of the Church and their brethren in faith and love: "If anyone claims to serve, let it be as by a command received from God" (1 Peter 4:11–12; cf. Romans 12:8; 1 Corinthians 12:5).

This diakonia done to others by Christians can take the form of different expressions of fraternal charity, service to the physically or spiritually sick, to the needy, to prisoners (Matthew 25); the help given to the churches (Romans 15:25; 1 Timothy 5:3–16); or different kinds of assistance given to apostles, as can be seen in the case of the men and women collaborators of Saint Paul, who sends them his greetings (Romans 16:3–5; Philippians 4:3).

II. DIAKONIA OF THE APOSTLES

Because he was the *doulos,* or slave, carrying out the Father's saving will in total obedience, Jesus Christ was made Lord of all creation. He made himself the instrument through which God's sovereignty was achieved, by giving his life: "The Son of Man has not come to be served but to serve, and to give his life as a ransom for many" (Mark 10:45). In the same way, Jesus instituted the Twelve "to be his companions and sent them out to preach, giving them the power to cast out demons" (Mark 3:14–15). In a way that was radically opposed to the lords and rulers of this world who abuse their power to oppress and exploit others, the disciple must be ready to become *diakonos* and *doulos* of all (Mark 10:42–43).

Diakonein, to serve, is the essential characteristic of the apostle's ministry. Apostles are collaborators and servants of God (cf. 1 Thessalonians 3:2; 1 Corinthians 3:9; 2 Corinthians 6:1), "servants of Christ and witnesses of God's mysteries" (1 Corinthians 4:1). They are "ministers of a new covenant" (2 Corinthians 3:6) and ministers of the Gospel (cf. Colossians 1:23; Ephesians 3:6 ff.), "servants of the word" (Acts of the Apostles 6:4). They are, in their function as apostles, "ministers of the Church" in order to bring about the coming of the word of Christ in its fullness to believers (cf. Colossians 1:25), and to organize the building up of the Church, the Body of Christ, in love (cf. Ephesians 4:12). The apostles become the servants of believers because of Christ, since it is not themselves whom they are proclaiming, but Christ Jesus the Lord (2 Corinthians 4:5). They are sent in the name of Christ, the word having been passed on to them so that they may proclaim it in the service of reconciliation. Through them, God himself *exhorts* and *acts* in the Holy Spirit and in Christ Jesus, who has reconciled the world with him (cf. 2 Corinthians 5:20).

III. Diakonia of the Apostles' Collaborators

Within the Pauline communities, with, as well as, or after Saint Paul,
Saint Peter and the other eleven apostles (cf. 1 Corinthians 15:3–5;
Galatians 2), are to be found direct collaborators with Saint Paul in
the apostolic ministry (for example, Sylvanus, Timothy, Titus, Apollos)
as well as many others allied to him in apostolic activities and service
to local churches (2 Corinthians 8:23). These include Epaphroditus
(Philippians 2:25), Epaphras (Colossians 4:12) and Archippus
(Colossians 4:17), who are named as servants of Christ. In the opening
words of the Epistle to the Philippians (around 50 AD) Saint Paul
sends a special greeting to "their bishops and their deacons"
(Philippians 1:1). This necessarily calls to mind the ministries
that were then taking shape in the Church.

It is of course recognized that the terminology of these
ministries was not yet fixed. Reference is made to the *proistamenoi*
(Romans 12:8) "who are at your head in the Lord and who reprimand
you," and whom the Thessalonians are to hold "in extreme charity,
by reason of their work" (1 Thessalonians 5:12); reference is also made
to leaders (*hegoumenoi*), "who have made you hear the word of God";
the Epistle to the Hebrews adds, "Obey your leaders and be docile
to them" (13:7.17; cf. 13:24; cf. 1 Clem 1:3; 21:6); and reference is made
to the "men who were sent" who guide the communities (cf. Acts of
the Apostles 15:22), to apostles, prophets, and teachers (cf. 1 Corinthians
12:28; Galatians 6:6; Acts of the Apostles 13:1; 4:14), and to
"evangelists, or rather shepherds and teachers" (Ephesians 4:11).
Saint Paul says of Stephanas, Fortunatus, and Achaicus, "the first-fruits
of Achaia," "that they spontaneously put themselves at the service
of the saints" (1 Corinthians 16:15); and he exhorts the Corinthians:
"Place yourselves under such men, and under whoever works and
labors with them" (1 Corinthians 16:16).

The activity expressed in these terms points to the official
titles that were to take shape soon afterward. It is clear from these
documents that the early Church attributed the formation of the
various ministries to the action of the Holy Spirit (1 Corinthians 12:28;
Ephesians 4:11; Acts of the Apostles 20:28) and to the personal initia-
tive of the apostles, who owed their sending forth on their mission to
the Most High and Lord of this world, and who anchored their role of

upholding the Church in the power they had received from him
(Mark 3:13–19; 6:6–13; Matthew 28:16–20; Acts of the Apostles
1:15–26; Galatians 1:10–24).

    Diakonein is shown to be a radical determination of *Christian life*, expressing itself in the sacramental basis of Christian existence, of the charismatic building up of the Church, and also of the sending out of the apostles on their mission and of the *ministry* that flows from the apostolate, of the proclamation of the Gospel, and of the sanctification and governance of churches.

Chapter 2

The Diaconate in the New Testament and in the Writings of the Fathers

I. The Diaconate in the New Testament

1. Difficulties in terminology

The word *diakonos* is almost absent from the Old Testament by contrast with *presbyteros*, which is abundantly used. In the Septuagint, in the rare places where the word *diakonos* is attested, it means messenger or servant.[1] The Latin Bible (Vulgate) renders it in a general sense by *minister* or, in a specific sense, by transliterating the Greek word to give *diaconus*. But the terms *minister*, *ministerium*, and *ministrare* are also used to render other Greek terms, such as *hyperetes* and *leitourgos*. In the Vulgate the use of *diaconus* is found three times,[2] and in the remaining cases the word is translated to *minister*.[3]

Apart from the words *diakoneo*, *diakonia*, and *diakonos*, Greek could choose between the following words: *douleuo* (to serve as a servant), *therapeuo* (someone who volunteers to serve), *latreuo* (to serve for wages), *leitourgeo* (someone who holds public office), and *hypereteo* (governor).[4] In any case, it is characteristic that the verbal form *diakonein* is unknown in the Septuagint, the functions of service being translated by the verbs *leitourgein* or *latreuein*. Philo only used it in the sense of "to serve."[5] Josephus knew it in the sense of "to serve," "to obey" and "priestly service."[6] In the New Testament, the word *douleuo* meant service of a very personal kind: the service of charity. In the language of the Gospels[7] and at Acts of the Apostles 6:2, *diakoneo* means "ministering at table." Making a collection whose proceeds Paul would take to Jerusalem was a service of this kind.[8] The apostle goes to Jerusalem for "a ministry to the saints."[9]

As for the use of the words *cheirotonia, cheirotesia, ordinatio,* there is a degree of uncertainty with regard to these terms.[10]

2. Data from the New Testament

The first fundamental fact of relevance from the New Testament is that the verb *diakonein* designates Christ's actual mission as servant (Mark 10:45 and parallels; cf. Matthew 12:18; Acts of the Apostles 4:30; Philippians 2:6–11). This word or its derivatives also designates the exercise of service or ministry by his disciples (Mark 10:43ff.; Matthew 20:26ff.; 23:11; Luke 8:3; Romans 15:25), the ministries of different kinds in the Church, especially the apostolic ministry of preaching the Gospel, and other charismatic gifts.[11]

The words *diakonein* and *diakonos* are widely used, with a wide range of meanings, in the language of the New Testament.[12]

The *diakonos* may mean the servant who waits at table (e. g. John 2:5 and 9), the servant of the Lord (Matthew 22:13; John 12:26; Mark 9:35; 10:43; Matthew 20:26; 23:11), the servant of a spiritual power (2 Corinthians 11:14; Ephesians 3:6; Colossians 1:23; Galatians 2:17; Romans 15:8; 2 Corinthians 3:6), the servant of the Gospel, of Christ or of God (2 Corinthians 11:23). Pagan authorities are also in the service of God (Romans 13:4); the deacons are the servants of the Church (Colossians 1:25; 1 Corinthians 3:5). In the case where the deacon belongs to one of the Churches, the Vulgate does not use the word *minister* but retains the Greek word *diaconus.*[13] This fact shows clearly that in Acts of the Apostles 6:1–6 it is not the institution of the diaconate that is being referred to.[14]

"Diaconate" and "apostolate" are sometimes synonymous, as in Acts of the Apostles 1:17–25, where, on the occasion of the addition of Matthias to the eleven apostles, Peter calls the apostolate "a share in our service" (v. 17: *ton kleron tes diakonias tautes*) and speaks of service and apostolate (v. 25: *ton topon tes diakonias kai apostoles,* which is sometimes translated as "the service of the apostolate.") This text from Acts also quotes Psalm 109:8, "Let another take over his position (*ten episkopen*)." The question therefore arises as to whether *diakonia, apostole,* and *episkope* are equivalent to each other or not. In the opinion of M. J. Schmitt and J. Colson, "apostolate" is "an editorial term correcting diakonias."[15]

Acts of the Apostles 6:1–6 describes the institution of the "Seven"[16] "to serve at tables." The reason for this is given by Luke as stemming from internal tensions within the community: "the Hellenists complained (*egeneto goggysmos*) against the Hebrews because their widows were being neglected in the daily distribution of food" (Acts of the Apostles 6:1). It has not yet been ascertained whether the widows of the "Hellenists" belonged to the community or not, according to strict respect for ritual purity. Were the apostles hoping to send to the provinces the rebellious "Hellenists" of Jerusalem who, in their preaching in the synagogue, were responsible for much provocation? Is this why the apostles chose "Seven," which was the number of provincial community magistrates attached to a synagogue? But at the same time, through the imposition of hands, they wished to preserve the unity of the Spirit and avoid a schism.[17] Commentators on Acts do not explain the significance of this laying-on of the apostles' hands.

It is possible that the apostles appointed the Seven to be at the head of the "Hellenists" (baptized Greek-speaking Jews) to fulfill the same task as the presbyters among the "Hebrew" Christians.[18]

The reason given for the designation of the chosen Seven (complaints by the Hellenists) is in contradiction with their actual activity as later described by Luke. We hear nothing about serving at tables. Out of the Seven, Luke only speaks of the activities of Stephen and Philip; or more precisely, Stephen's discourse in the synagogue at Jerusalem, and his martyrdom, and the apostolate carried out in Samaria by Philip, who also baptized people.[19] There is no word of the others.[20]

In the churches entrusted to Saint Paul's apostolic care, deacons appear beside the *episkopoi* as exercising a ministry subordinate to or coordinated with theirs (Philippians 1:1; 1 Timothy 3:1–13). In the apostolic writings, mention is often made of deacons with the bishop, or else of the bishop with priests. However, historical sources which cite all three together, bishop, priest, and deacon, are very rare.

II. THE APOSTOLIC FATHERS

The first epistle of Saint Clement of Rome to the Corinthians (first century) mentions that the bishops and deacons have a spiritual function in the community: "The apostles received for us the good news through the Lord Jesus Christ; Jesus, the Christ, was sent by

God. Therefore the Christ comes from God, the apostles come from Christ; both proceeded in due order from the will of God (*egenonto oun amphotera eutaktos ek thelematos Theou*). They therefore received instructions and, filled with conviction by the Resurrection of our Lord Jesus Christ, strengthened by the word of God, with the full conviction of the Holy Spirit, they set out to announce the good news of the coming of God's kingdom. They preached in the countryside and in the towns and they established (*kathistanon*) its firstfruits, they tested them by the Spirit, so as to make them bishops and deacons (*eis episkopous kai diakonous*) of those who were to believe. And there was nothing new (*o u kainos*) in this; for long ago scripture spoke of bishops and deacons (*egegrapto peri episkopon kai diakonon*); for it is written somewhere, 'I shall establish their bishops in justice and their deacons in faith'."[21]

When the author of the Epistle of Clement speaks of liturgical functions, he refers to the Old Testament;[22] when he explains the institution of the *episkopoi kai diakonoi*, he refers to the will of God, and to the apostles.[23] The order of bishops and deacons was not an innovation, but was founded on the will of God, and therefore was a "due order"; their sending originated in God himself. The successors chosen by the apostles were the firstfruits offered to God. The apostles had tested the chosen ones by the Spirit; those who succeeded them would be established by the choice of the whole assembly.[24] Here we find the tradition of the pastoral letters in reverse order: (1) the testing in the Spirit (cf. 1 Timothy 3:1–7 and 8:10ff.); (2) the use side-by-side of the terms *episkopos kai diakonos* (cf. Philippians 1:1), where *episkopos* does not yet correspond to the present definition of bishop.[25] It is worth noting the way Saint Polycarp linked the ministry of deacons with the service of Christ the Savior: "let them walk in the truth of the Lord who became the servant (*diakonos*) of all" (Letter of Saint Polycarp to the Philippians 5, 2).

The text of the *Didache* (written before 130 AD) at 15, 1 only mentions bishops and deacons as the successors of the prophets and the *didaskaloi*, and says nothing of priests: "Choose yourselves therefore bishops and deacons worthy of the Lord, mild men, fairminded, truthful and reliable, for they too fulfill toward you the offices of prophets and teachers."[26] J.-P. Audet comments, "The two words

admittedly sound different to us. But in Greek, at the time of the
Didache, an *episkopos* was a supervisor, foreman, guardian, moderator,
warden or steward . . . Whereas a *diakonos* was simply a servant
able to fulfill different functions according to the particular conditions
of his service. The two terms are widely used with a variety of
meanings . . . The specific way they were appointed (*cheirotonesate*)
remains unclear. They were chosen and appointed, perhaps by election;
that is all that can be said."[27] The Didache does not say anything about
ordination. According to K. Niederwimmer, the term *cheirotonein*
means election.[28]

It is certain that at that period the deacons were responsible
for the life of the Church with regard to works of charity toward
widows and orphans, as was the case in the first community at Jerusalem.
Their activities were doubtless linked to catechesis and also probably
to the liturgy. However information on this subject is so brief[29]
that it is difficult to learn from it the precise range of their functions.

The letters of Saint Ignatius of Antioch point to a new stage.
His statements about the ecclesiastical hierarchy with its three grades
are similar to those of Clement of Rome: "Let everyone revere the
deacons as Jesus Christ, the bishop as the image of the Father, and the
presbyters as the senate of God and the assembly of the apostles. For
without them one cannot speak of the Church."[30] And again, "All
of you, follow the bishop, as Jesus Christ [follows] his Father, and the
presbyterium as the apostles; as for the deacons, respect them as the
law of God."[31] Saint Ignatius speaks of the bishop in the singular
and of priests and deacons in the plural, but says nothing on the
character of the diaconate, simply exhorting the faithful to venerate
the deacons as appointed by God.

Saint Justin († 165) gives information especially about the
liturgical activity of deacons. He describes the role of deacons in the
Eucharist during the *oblatio* and the *communio*: "Then there is brought
to him who presides over the assembly of the brethren, some bread
and a cup of water and wine mixed . . . once the prayers and giving of
thanks are over, all the people present express their assent by replying
Amen . . . When the president of the assembly has finished the
prayer of thanksgiving (eucharist) and all the people have made their
response, those who among us are called deacons (*oi kaloumenoi par
'emin diakonoi*) give to each of those present to share in the bread and

in the wine mixed with water over which has been said the prayer
of thanksgiving (eucharist), and they carry it to those who are absent."[32]

III. Consolidation and Development of the Diaconate in the Third and Fourth Centuries

According to Clement of Alexandria there are in the Church, as in
the life of civil society, positions that are intended to benefit either
the body or the soul (*therapeia beltiotike, hyperetike*). There are also
people who in themselves are ordered to the service of people of
a higher grade. Priests are of the first kind and deacons of the second.[33]
In Origen, the *diakonia* of the bishop is always the service of the whole
Church (*ekklesiastike diakonia*). The bishop is called "prince" and, at
the same time, also called "servant of all."[34] Deacons are often criticized
by Origen because they are particularly infected by the spirit of
covetousness. Because of their responsibility for charitable works, they
were more in contact with money. In a passage on the expulsion of the
traders from the Temple, Origen speaks of those "deacons who do
not administer rightly the tables of the money of the Church (*sc.* of the
poor), but always act fraudulently toward them."[35] "They amass riches
for themselves, misappropriating money meant for the poor."[36]

The *Didascalia* (third century) evidences a degree of
supremacy of deacons over priests, since deacons are compared to
Christ, while priests are only compared to the apostles.[37] But in the
first place, priests are presented as the senate of the Church and the
bishop's assessors; they are placed around the altar and the episcopal
throne. The deacons are called the "third ones," which probably
suggests that they come after the bishop and the priests. However, the
status and activity of deacons undoubtedly seem to have surpassed
those of priests. The laity ought to have great confidence in the deacons
and not importune the head, but make their wishes known to him
through the *hyperetai*, that is through the deacons, for no one can
approach the almighty Lord and God either except through Christ.[38]
In the *Didascalia* the increase in the status of the diaconate in
the Church is remarkable, resulting in a growing crisis in the reciprocal
relations of priests and deacons. To the deacons' social and charitable

responsibilities was added that of providing various services during liturgical assemblies: ushering in newcomers and pilgrims; taking care of the offerings; supervising orderliness and silence; and ensuring that people were suitably dressed.

The *Traditio Apostolica* of Hippolytus of Rome († 235) presents the theological and juridical status of the deacon in the Church for the first time. It includes them among the group of the *ordinati* by the imposition of hands (*cheirotonein*), contrasting them with those in the hierarchy who are called *instituti*. The "ordination" of deacons is done only by the bishop (Chapter 8). This connection defines the scope of the tasks of the deacon, who is at the disposition of the bishop, to fulfill his orders but is excluded from taking part in the council of priests.

A comparison should be made between the two texts for the ordination of deacons, that of the *Veronense* (L, Latin version) and that of the Sahidic Ethiopian (S[AE]), because there are some differences between them. L says: "Diaconus vero cum ordinatur, eligatur secundum ea, quae praedicta sunt, similiter imponens manus episcopus solus sicuti praecipimus." S[AE] is clearer: "Episcopus autem instituet (kathistasthai) diaconum qui electus est, secundum quod praedictum est." There is still, however, a difference between *ordinatio* and *institutio*. The tenth chapter, speaking of the widows of the *Traditio Apostolica* contributes some significant elements. "Non autem imponetur manus super eam, quia non offert oblationem neque habet liturgiam. Ordinatio (*cheirotonia*) autem fit cum clero (*kleros*) propter liturgiam. Vidua (*xera*) autem instituitur (*kathistasthai*) propter orationem: haec autem est omnium."[39] According to this text, if the imposition of hands is absent from the rite, then it is only an institution (*katastasis, institutio*) and not an *ordinatio*. Thus, in the course of the third century, the imposition of hands already constituted the distinctive sign of the rite of ordination to major orders. In the fourth century it was extended to minor orders as well.

In what concerns the liturgy, the task of the deacon was to bring the offerings and distribute them. In the administration of Baptism, his role was to accompany the priest and serve him "the oil of the catechumens and the chrism and also to go down into the water with the person who was to receive Baptism" (Chapter 21). Another field of work for the deacons was teaching: "Let them come together and instruct those with whom they are in the Church . . ."

(Chapter 39). Their social activity is emphasized, specifically in close union with the bishop.

According to Saint Cyprian, "The deacons should not forget that the Lord himself chose the apostles, that is, the bishops and the heads of the church, while in the case of deacons, it was the apostles who instituted them after the Lord's Ascension, to be ministers of their episcopate and of the Church. Hence, just as we cannot undertake anything in defiance of God who makes us bishops, neither can they too undertake anything in defiance of us, who make them deacons."[40] It seems that, from time to time, even at Carthage, the deacons wished to take the place of the priests. They had to be warned that deacons came in third place in the order of the hierarchy. While the see was vacant they also had an important role in the governance of the Church. In exile, Cyprian normally addressed his letters "to the priests and deacons" to discuss disciplinary problems. In Cyprian's writings, priests and deacons were sometimes designated by the word *clerus*, and less frequently were called *praepositi*.[41] The priest Gaius Didensis and his deacons were both charged to offer the Eucharist, but the fifth letter indicates that in reality it was the priests who offered it, attended by the deacons.[42] To deacons, on the other hand, falls the practice of charity by visiting those in prison. They are described as "boni viri et ecclesiasticae administrationis per omnia devoti."[43] The word *administratio* is found in the expression *sancta administratio* applied to the deacon Nicostratus in regard to the Church money that he looked after. Thus deacons would be charged not only with the practice of charity toward the poor, but also with the administration of the finances belonging to the community.[44]

To sum up, as well as the fact of the existence of the diaconate in all the Churches from the beginning of the second century and the fact of the ecclesiastical nature of the diaconate as such, it can be said that the role fulfilled by deacons was basically the same everywhere, although the emphasis placed on the various elements of their commitment may have differed in different regions. The diaconate was stabilized in the course of the fourth century. In the synodal and conciliar directives of this period the diaconate was regarded as an essential element of the hierarchy of the local Church. At the synod of Elvira (c. 306–309) the diaconate's preeminent role in the administrative sector of the Church was primarily underlined.

Paradoxically, at the same time as it imposed a certain limitation on the involvement of deacons in the liturgical sector, this synod attributed to them the possibility of giving absolution of sins in urgent cases. This tendency to invade the field of competences of priests, which was also manifested in the claim to preside at the Eucharist (albeit as an exception) was stopped to by the synod of Arles (314) and particularly by the Council of Nicaea (325, can. 18).

The *Constitutiones Apostolorum* (CA), which forms the most impressive of the juridical collections drawn up in the fourth century, cites the different parts of the *Didache* and the *Didascalia* which refer to deacons, and comments on them in ways that reflect the point of view of the period. Also included are the statements of Saint Ignatius in his letters, thus providing a considerable amount of information. The text is characterized by a tendency to historicism, the more so since the author-editor looks for prefigurations in parallel passages of the Old Testament. He introduces his discourse with a solemn formula (cf. Deuteronomy 5:31 and 27:9): "Hear, O sacred and catholic Church . . . For these are your pontiffs; your priests are the presbyters, and your Levites are now the deacons, these are your lectors, cantors and door-keepers, these are your deaconesses, your widows, your virgins and your orphans . . . The deacon will attend him as Christ attends the Father . . ."[45] He describes the relation of the bishop with the deacon through the prefigurations of the old Covenant and the heavenly models: "For you now, Aaron is the deacon and Moses the bishop; if therefore Moses was called a god by the Lord, among you the bishop shall be likewise honored as a god and the deacon as his prophet . . . and as the Son is the angel and prophet of the Father, in the same way the deacon is the angel and prophet of the bishop."[46] The deacon represents the eye, the ear, and the mouth of the bishop "so that the bishop does not have to concern himself with a multitude of matters, but only with the most important ones, as Jethro established for Moses, and his counsel was well received."[47] The prayer of ordination of a deacon by the bishop attests that the diaconate was envisaged as a transitory grade toward the presbyterate: "Grant that he may satisfactorily accomplish the service which has been entrusted to him, in a seemly manner, without deviation or blame or reproach, to be judged worthy of a higher rank (*meizonos axiothenai bathmou*), through the mediation of your Christ, your only-begotten Son . . ."[48]

In the *Euchologion* of Serapion (toward the end of the fourth century) there appears a prayer of ordination of a deacon whose terminology is similar to that of the Sahidic version of the *Traditio Apostolica*. The text of the prayer alludes to the canons of the Church, to the three hierarchical grades, and refers to the Seven in Acts chapter 6; to designate the ordination of the deacon it employs the verb *katisthanai:* "Pater unigeniti, qui *filium misisti* tuum et ordinasti res super terra atque ecclesiae canones et ordines dedisti in utilitatem et salutem gregum, qui elegisti episcopos et presbyteros et diaconos in ministerium catholicae tuae ecclesiae, qui elegisti per unigenitum tuum septem diaconos eisque largitus es spiritum sanctum: constitue (*katasteson*) et hunc diaconum ecclesiae tuae catholicae et da in eo *spiritum cognitionis ac discretionis*, ut possit inter populum sanctum pure et immaculate ministrare in hoc ministerio per unigenitum tuum Iesum Christum, per quem tibi gloriam et imperium in sancto spiritu et nunc et in omnia saecula saeculorum, amen."[49]

The prayer of consecration of a deacon in the *Sacramentarium Veronense* speaks of the service of the holy altar, and, like the text in the *Constitutiones Apostolorum*, considers the diaconate to be a transitory grade. "Oremus . . . quos consecrationis indultae propitius dona conservet . . . quos ad officium levitarum vocare dignaris, altaris sancti ministerium tribuas sufficienter implere . . . trinis gradibus ministrorum nomini tuo militare constituens . . . dignisque successibus de inferiori gradu per gratiam tuam capere potiora mereantur."[50] The *Sacramentarium Gregorianum* is similar at every point to the texts already cited. It also recalls the three grades, and uses the word *"constituere"* to designate the ordination of the deacon.[51]

Behind their apparent unanimity, the declarations of the Fathers of the Church in the fourth century give a glimpse of certain dissensions which had been well known since the third century, as for example the deacons' claim to appropriate the places, rank, and tasks of the priests.[52]

There is also evidence of the idea that the three grades (bishop, priest and deacon) were like elements of one and the same order. Pseudo-Athanasios speaks of this in his work *De Trinitate* as a "consubstantiality."[53] In addition, Christianity was beginning to spread in provincial areas, with bishops or priests leaving the town against their will, and deacons doing so very willingly, but abusing the situation in that they used to appropriate certain of priests' rights. The historical context also contributed to this development. What had happened was that the Arians had compromised the standing of the episcopate. Contrasting with bishops and priests avid for power and money, the popularity of deacons grew strongly because of their close links with monks and laypeople. The widespread opinion in the fourth century was that deacons had been instituted by the apostles and the bishop ordained them in the same way as priests. Deacons belonged to the clergy but only assisted at the liturgy.[54]

The sources show us that even Chrysostom did not manage to place the three grades of the ecclesial order in a clear historical continuity. There were Jewish models for the priesthood, but the episcopate and diaconate were instituted by the apostles. It is not clear what should be understood by these notions.[55] Chrysostom stated that the diaconate had been instituted by the Holy Spirit.[56] In the course of this century, the Latins also took up the use of the Greek word "diaconus," as Saint Augustine attests.[57]

The fourth century marked the end of the process which led to the recognition of the diaconate as a grade or degree in the ecclesial hierarchy, placed after the bishop and the priests, with a well-defined role. Linked to the bishop himself and his mission, this role encompassed three tasks: the service of the liturgy, the service of preaching the Gospel and teaching catechesis, and a vast social activity concerning the works of charity and administrative action in accordance with the bishop's directives.

IV. The Ministry of Deaconesses

In the apostolic era different forms of diaconal assistance offered to the apostles and communities by women seem to have been institutional. Thus Paul recommends to the community at Rome "our sister Phoebe, servant (*he diakonos*) of the Church at Cenchreae" (cf. Romans 16:1–4). Although the masculine form of *diakonos* is used here, it cannot therefore be concluded that the word is being used to designate the specific function of a "deacon"; first because in this context *diakonos* still signifies servant in a very general sense, and second because the word "servant" is not given a feminine suffix but preceded by a feminine article. What seems clear is that Phoebe exercised a recognized service in the community of Cenchreae, subordinate to the ministry of the apostle. Elsewhere in Paul's writings the authorities of the world are themselves called *diakonos* (Romans 13:4) and in 2 Corinthians 11:14–15, he refers to *diakonoi* of the devil.

Exegetes are divided on the subject of 1 Timothy 3:11. The mention of "women" following the reference to deacons may suggest women deacons (by parallel reference), or the deacons' wives who had been mentioned earlier. In this epistle, the functions of the deacon are not described, but only the conditions for admitting them. It is said that women must not teach or rule over men (1 Timothy 2:8–15). But the functions of governance and teaching were in any case reserved to the bishop (1 Timothy 3:5) and to priests (1 Timothy 5:17), and not to deacons. Widows constituted a recognized group in the community, from whom they received assistance in exchange for their commitment to continence and prayer. 1 Timothy 5:3–16 stresses the conditions under which they may be inscribed on the list of widows receiving relief from the community, and says nothing more about any functions they might have. Later on they were officially "instituted" but "not ordained";[58] they constituted an "order" in the Church[59] and would never have any other mission apart from good example and prayer. At the beginning of the second century, a letter from Pliny the Younger, governor of Bithynia, mentioned two women who were described by the Christians as *ministrae,* the probable equivalent of the Greek diakonoi (X 96–97). It was not until the third century that the specific Christian terms *diaconissa* or *diacona* appeared.

From the end of the third century onward, in certain regions of the Church[60] (and not all of them), a specific ecclesial ministry is attested to on the part of women called deaconesses.[61] This was in Eastern Syria and Constantinople. Toward 240 there appeared a singular canonico-liturgical compilation, the *Didascalia Apostolorum* (DA), which was not official in character. It attributed to the bishop the features of an omnipotent biblical patriarch (cf. DA 2, 33–35, 3). He was at the head of a little community which he governed mainly with the help of deacons and deaconesses. This was the first time that deaconesses appeared in an ecclesiastical document. In a typology borrowed from Ignatius of Antioch, the bishop held the place of God the Father, the deacon the place of Christ, and the deaconess that of the Holy Spirit (the word for "Spirit" is feminine in Semitic languages), while the priests (who are seldom mentioned) represented the apostles, and the widows, the altar (DA 2, 26, 4–7). There is no reference to the ordination of these ministers.

The *Didascalia* laid stress on the charitable role of the deacon and the deaconess. The ministry of the diaconate should appear as "one single soul in two bodies." Its model is the diakonia of Christ, who washed the feet of his disciples (DA 3, 13, 1–7). However, there was no strict parallelism between the two branches of the diaconate with regard to the functions they exercised. The deacons were chosen by the bishop to "concern themselves about many necessary things," and the deaconesses only "for the service of women" (DA 3, 12, 1). The hope was expressed that "the number of deacons may be proportionate to that of the assembly of the people of the Church" (DA 3, 13, 1).[62] The deacons administered the property of the community in the bishop's name. Like the bishop, they were maintained at its expense. Deacons are called the ear and mouth of the bishop (DA 2, 44, 3–4). Men from among the faithful should go through the deacons to have access to the bishop, as women should go through the deaconesses (DA 3, 12, 1–4). One deacon supervised the entries into the meetingplace, while another attended the bishop for the Eucharistic offering (DA 2, 57, 6).

Deaconesses should carry out the anointing of women in the Rite of Baptism, instruct women neophytes, and visit the women faithful, especially the sick, in their homes. They were forbidden to confer Baptism themselves, or to play a part in the Eucharistic offering (DA 3, 12, 1–4). The deaconesses had supplanted the widows. The bishop may still institute widows, but they should not either teach or administer Baptism (to women), but only pray (DA 3, 5, 1–3, 6, 2).

The *Constitutiones Apostolorum*, which appeared in Syria toward 380, used and interpolated the *Didascalia*, the *Didache* and the *Traditio Apostolica*. The *Constitutiones* were to have a lasting influence on the discipline governing ordinations in the East, even though they were never considered to be an official canonical collection. The compiler envisaged the imposition of hands with the epiklesis of the Holy Spirit not only for bishops, priests and deacons but also for the deaconesses, subdeacons and lectors (cf. CA VIII 16–23).[63] The concept of *klèros* was broadened to all those who exercised a liturgical ministry, who were maintained by the Church, and who benefited from the privileges in civil law allowed by the Empire to clerics, so that the deaconesses were counted as belonging to the clergy, while the widows were excluded. Bishop and priests were paralleled with the high priest and the priests respectively of the Old Covenant, while to the Levites corresponded all the other ministries and states of life: "deacons, lectors, cantors, door-keepers, deaconesses, widows, virgins and orphans" (CA II 26, 3. CA VIII 1, 21). The deacon was placed "at the service of the bishop and the priests" and should not impinge on the functions of the latter.[64] The deacon could proclaim the Gospel and conduct the prayer of the assembly (CA II 57, 18), but only the bishop and the priests exhorted (CA II 57, 7). Deaconesses took up their functions through an *epithesis cheirôn* or imposition of hands that conferred the Holy Spirit,[65] as did the lectors (CA VIII 20. 22). The bishop pronounced the following prayer: "Eternal God, Father of our Lord Jesus Christ, creator of man and woman, who filled Myriam, Deborah, Anne and Hulda with your spirit; who did not deem it unworthy for your Son, the Only-Begotten, to be born of a woman; who in the tent of witness and in the temple did institute women as guardians of your sacred doors, look now upon your servant before you, proposed for the diaconate: grant her the Holy Spirit and purify her of all defilement of flesh and spirit so that she may acquit herself worthily of the office which has been entrusted to her, for your glory and to the praise of your Christ, through whom be glory and adoration to you, in the Holy Spirit, world without end. Amen."[66]

The deaconesses were named before the subdeacon who, in his turn, received a *cheirotonia* like the deacon (CA VIII 21), while the virgins and widows could not be "ordained" (VIII 24–25). The *Constitutiones* insist that the deaconesses should have no liturgical function (III 9, 1–2), but should devote themselves to their function in the community which was "service to the women" (CA III 16, 1) and as intermediaries between women and the bishop. It is still stated that they represent the Holy Spirit, but they "do nothing without the deacon" (CA II 26, 6). They should stand at the women's entrances in the assemblies (II 57, 10). Their functions are summed up as follows: "The deaconess does not bless, and she does not fulfill any of the things that priests and deacons do, but she looks after the doors and attends the priests during the Baptism of women, for the sake of decency" (CA VIII 28, 6).

This is echoed by the almost contemporary observation of Epiphanius of Salamis in his *Panarion,* in around 375: "There is certainly in the Church the order of deaconesses, but this does not exist to exercise the functions of a priest, nor are they to have any undertaking committed to them, but for the decency of the feminine sex at the time of Baptism."[67] A law of Theodosius of 21 June 390, revoked on 23 August of the same year, fixed the age for admission to the ministry of deaconesses at 60. The Council of Chalcedon (can. 15) reduced the age to 40, forbidding them subsequent marriage.[68]

Even in the fourth century the way of life of deaconesses was very similar to that of nuns. At that time the woman in charge of a monastic community of women was called a deaconess, as is testified by Gregory of Nyssa among others.[69] Ordained abbesses of the monasteries of women, the deaconesses wore the maforion, or veil of perfection. Until the sixth century they still attended women in the baptismal pool and for the anointing. Although they did not serve at the altar, they could distribute communion to sick women. When the practice of anointing the whole body at Baptism was abandoned, deaconesses were simply consecrated virgins who had taken the vow of chastity. They lived either in monasteries or at home. The condition for admission was virginity or widowhood and their activity consisted of charitable and health-related assistance to women.

At Constantinople the best-known of the fourth-century deaconesses was Olympias, the superior of a monastery of women, who was a protégée of Saint John Chrysostom and had put her property at the service of the Church. She was "ordained" (*cheirotonein*) deaconess with three of her companions by the patriarch. Can. 15 of the Council of Chalcedon (451) seems to confirm the fact that deaconesses really were "ordained" by the imposition of hands (*cheirotonia*). Their ministry was called *leitourgia* and after ordination they were not allowed to marry.

In eighth-century Byzantium, the bishop still imposed his hands on a deaconess, and conferred on her the orarion or stole (both ends of which were worn at the front, one over the other); he gave her the chalice, which she placed on the altar without giving

communion to anyone. Deaconesses were ordained in the course
of the Eucharistic liturgy, in the sanctuary, like deacons.[70] Despite the
similarities between the rites of ordination, deaconesses did not have
access to the altar or to any liturgical ministry. These ordinations were
intended mainly for the superiors of monasteries of women.

It should be pointed out that in the West there is no trace of
any deaconesses for the first five centuries. The *Statuta Ecclesiae antiqua*
laid down that the instruction of women catechumens and their
preparation for Baptism was to be entrusted to the widows and
women religious "chosen *ad ministerium baptizandarum mulierum.*"[71]
Certain councils of the fourth and fifth centuries reject every
ministerium feminae[72] and forbid any ordination of deaconesses.[73]
According to the *Ambrosiaster* (composed at Rome at the end of the
fourth century), the female diaconate was an adjunct of Montanist
("Cataphrygian") heretics.[74] In the sixth century women admitted into
the group of widows were sometimes referrred to as deaconesses.
To prevent any confusion, the Council of Epaone forbade "the conse-
crations of widows who call themselves deaconesses."[75] The second
Council of Orleans (533) decided to exclude from communion women
who had "received the blessing for the diaconate despite the canons
forbidding this and who had remarried."[76] Abbesses, or the wives
of deacons, were also called *diaconissae*, by analogy with *presbyterissae*
or even *episcopissae.*[77]

The present historical overview shows that a ministry of
deaconesses did indeed exist, and that this developed unevenly in the
different parts of the Church. It seems clear that this ministry was not
perceived as simply the feminine equivalent of the masculine
diaconate. At the very least it was an ecclesial function, exercised by
women, sometimes mentioned together with that of subdeacon in the
lists of Church ministries.[78] Was this ministry conferred by an
imposition of hands comparable to that by which the episcopate, the
priesthood and the masculine diaconate were conferred? The text of
the *Constitutiones Apostolorum* would seem to suggest this, but it is
practically the only witness to this, and its proper interpretation is the
subject of much debate.[79] Should the imposition of hands on
deaconesses be considered the same as that on deacons, or is it rather
on the same level as the imposition of hands on subdeacons and

lectors? It is difficult to tackle the question on the basis of historical data alone. In the following chapters some elements will be clarified, and some questions will remain open. In particular, one chapter will be devoted to examining more closely how the Church through her theology and magisterium has become more conscious of the sacramental reality of Holy Orders and its three grades. But first it is appropriate to examine the causes which led to the disappearance of the permanent diaconate in the life of the Church.

---

1. Neh 1:10 "They are your servants and your people, whom you redeemed by your great power and your strong hand"; 6:3 "I sent messengers to them, saying . . ."; 6:5 "Sanballat . . . sent his servant to me . . ."; Proverbs 10:4a (Septuagint); 1M 11:58; 4M 9:17; Esther (Greek) 6:13.

2. Philippians 1:1; 1 Timothy 3:8.12.

3. Cf. E. Cattaneo, *I ministeri nella chiesa antica, testi patristici dei primi tre secoli*, Milan 1997, 33ff; J. Lecuyer, *Le sacrament de l'ordination* (ThH 65), Paris 1983, 131.

4. H. W. Beyer, *diakoneo, diakonia, diakonos*, in: ThWNT, Bd. II, 81–93.

5. *De vita contemplativa* 70 and 75.

6. *Antiquitates* VII 365; X 72.

7. Luke 17:8; 12:37; 22:26; John 12:2.

8. 2 Corinthians 8:19.

9. Romans 15:25.

10. "The meaning of the laying on of the hands in Acts of the Apostles 6:6 and 13:3 has been much disputed, but the stress laid on this gesture in both texts makes it difficult to see it as a mere act of blessing and not as an ordination rite . . . The usual verb to denote the election of a minister by the community is *eklegein*, Latin *eligere*. The verb *cheirotonein* may have the same meaning, 'to choose by stretching out the hand' (Did. 15,1), but it becomes a technical term for the appointment, i. e., the ordination of a minister, in Latin *ordinare*. In this meaning it is synonymous with *kathistanai*, Latin *instituere*. Another synonym is *procheirizein*. It is less usual and sometimes denotes the aspect of election and appointment by God. All these verbs are synonymous with *cheira(s) epitheinai*, but whereas the former group denotes the juridical aspect, the latter lays emphasis on the liturgical act. Moreover all the terms of the former group can be used for an appointment/ordination which does not include an imposition of hands, but there is apparently a preference for

cheirotonein / *cheirotonia*, as they are composed with *cheir-*, when the imposition of the hand (or of both hands) is included. A first attempt for such a distinction is made by Hippolytus, *Trad. A* 10." J. Ysebaert, *The Deaconesses in the Western Church of late Antiquity and their Origin*, in: *Eulogia*, Mélanges offertes à Antoon A. R. Bastiaensen (IP XXIV), Steenburgis 1991, 423.

11. Romans 11:13; 12:6ff; 1 Corinthians 12:5; 2 Corinthians 4:1; Ephesians 4:11ff; Hebrews 1:14: "leitourgika pneumata"; Acts of the Apostles 21:19; Colossians 4:17.

12. "Amt im Sinne Jesu muss immer 'diakonia' sein; nicht zufällig, nicht nebenbei, sondern sehr bewusst und ausdrücklich wählt die Heilige Schrift dieses Wort zu seiner Wesensbestimmung. Die griechische Sprache bot eine ganze Reihe von Möglichkeiten, das Amt in einer menschlichen Gemeinschaft—auch im religiös-kultischen Bereich—zu charakterisieren (archai, exousiai, archontes). Das Neue Testament wählte keine davon, sondern entschied sich für eine Bezeichnung, die weder in der jüdischen, noch in der hellenistischen Umwelt üblich war." E. Dassmann, *Ämter und Dienste in der frühchristlichen Gemeinden* (Hereditas 8), Bonn 1994, 37.

13. Philippians 1:1 "cum episcopis et diaconis"; 1 Timothy 3:8.12 "diaconos similiter . . . (sicut episcopi) diaconi sint . . ."

14. "Dieser Tatbestand zeigt, dass der Ursprung des Diakonenamtes nicht in Ag 6 zu finden ist . . . Der Diakonos ist nicht nur Diener seiner Gemeinde, sondern auch seines Bischofes." H. W. Beyer, *ibidem*, 90. Cf. M. Dibelius, *Bischöfe und Diakonen in Philippi (1937). Das kirchliche Amt im Neuen Testament* (WdF CDXXXIX), Darmstadt 1977, 413ff.; E. Schweizer, *Das Amt. Zum Amtsbegriff im Neuen Testament*, in: *Gemeinde und Gemeindeordnung im Neuen Testament* (AThANT 35), Zürich 1955, 154–164: "Als allgemeine Bezeichnung dessen, was wir 'Amt' nennen, also des Dienstes Einzelner innerhalb der Gemeinde, gibt es mit wenigen Ausnahmen nur ein einziges Wort: 'diakonia,' Diakonie. Das NT wählt also durchwegs und einheitlich ein Wort, das völlig unbiblisch und unreligiös ist und nirgends eine Assoziation mit einer besonderen Würde oder Stellung einschliesst. Im griechischen AT kommt das Wort nur einmal rein profan vor. . . . In der griechischen Sprachentwicklung ist die Grundbedeutung 'zu Tischen dienen' auch zum umfassenden Begriff 'dienen' ausgeweitet worden. Es bezeichnet fast durchwegs etwas Minderwertiges, kann aber im Hellenismus auch die Haltung des Weisen gegen Gott (nicht gegen den Mitmenschen) umschreiben"; K. H. Schelke, *Dienste und Diener in den Kirchen der Neutestamentlichen Zeit*, in: Concilium 5 (1969) 158–164; J. Brosch, *Charismen und Amter in der Urkirche*, Bonn 1951. Cf. B. Kötting, *Ämt und Verfassung in der Alten Kirche. Ecclesia peregrinans, Das Gottesvolk unterwegs* I (METh 54, 1), Münster1988, 429; G. Schöllgen, *Die Anfänge der Professionalisierung des Klerus und das kirchliche Amt in derd Syrischen Didaskalie* (JAC, Ergbd 26), Münster 1998, 93.

15. Cf. J. Colson, *Ministre de Jésus-Christ ou le Sacerdoce de l'Évangile* (ThH 4), Paris 1966, 191.

16. It was Irenaeus of Lyons (Adv. Haer. 3, 12, 10) who first referred to the "Seven" as "deacons."

17. "Die Siebenzahl wohl nach Analogie der sieben Mitglieder, aus denen in den jüdischen Gemeinden meist der Ortsvorstand sich zusammensetzte. Dieser hiess deshalb geradezu 'die Sieben einer Stadt' oder 'die Sieben Besten einer Stadt', während seine einzelnen Mitglieder . . . 'Hirten' oder 'Vorsteher' genannt wurden." H. L. Strack-Billerbeck, *Kommentar zum Neuen Testament aus Talmud und Midrasch,* Bd. II, Munich 1969, 641.

18. E. Haenchen, *Die Apostelgeschichte,* Neu übersetzt und erklärt, 12. neubearb. Auflage, Kritisch-exegetischer Kommentar, Göttingen 1959, 228–222; E. Dassmann, *Ämter und Dienste in den frühchristlichen Gemeinden* (Hereditas 8), Bonn 1994, 232: "Uber die Entstehung des Diakonenamtes sind keine genauere Angaben bekannt, seitdem feststeht, dass Apg 6 nicht die Bestellung von Diakonen, sondern von Beauftragten für die griechisch sprechende Gruppe der Urgemeinde beschreibt."

19. Cf. Acts of the Apostles 8:12.26–40 and 21:8, where Philip is called "the evangelist." "The next day we left and came to Caesarea; and went into the house of Philip the evangelist, one of the seven (*Philippou tou euaggelistou, ontos ek ton epta*), and stayed with him."

20. "Nicolaitae autem magistrum quidem habent Nicolaum, unum ex VII qui primi ad diaconium ab apostolis ordinati sunt: qui indiscrete vivunt." AH I, 23; Harvey I, 214. Hippolytus, *Philosophomena* VII 36; Tertullian, *De praescriptione,* 33. For the opposing view, Clement of Alexandria, *Strom.* II 118, 3 and III 25, 5–26, 2.

21. Cf. Isaiah 60:17, where the Septuagint does not mention "deacons," which must be an addition by Saint Clement; cf. 1 Clement 42, 1–5; SCh 167, 173, 168–171.

22. Cf. 40, 1 and 41, 2–4.

23. J. Colson, *Ministre de Jésus-Christ ou le Sacerdoce de l'Évangile,* 228ff.

24. I Clement 44, 3; SCh 167, 172–173.

25. "Von den zwei erwähnten Ämtern, *episkopoi* und *diakonoi,* wurde das erste mit 'Episkopen' wiedergegeben, um das sehr missverständliche 'Bischöfe' zu vermeiden. Denn auf keinen Fall handelt es sich dabei um die Institution des Monepiskopats." H. E. Lona, *Der erste Clemensbrief. Kommentar zu den Apostolischen Vätern,* Göttingen 1998, 446. Cf. E. Dassmann, *Ämter und Dienste in den frühchristlichen Gemeinden,* 40.

26. J.-Audet, *La Didachè. Instructions des Apôtres,* Paris 1958, 241.

27. Ibid., 465.

28. "'*Cheirotonein*' heisst hier (natürlich) 'wählen' und nicht 'ernennen'."
Kommentar zu den Apostolischen Vätern, Die Didache, Göttingen 1989, 241.

29. *Did.* 14, 1–3; 15, 1.

30. *Letter to the Trallians,* 3, 1; SCh 10, 113.

31. *Letter to the Smyrnaeans,* 8, 1; SCh 10, 163.

32. *Apol.* 1, 65, 3–5. Saint Justin, *Apologies.* Introduction, texte critique,
traduction, commentaire et index par A. Wartelle, Paris 1987, 188–191.

33. *Strom.* VII, 1, 3; GCS 17, 6.

34. *Comm. in Mat.* 16:8; GCS 40, 496.

35. *Ibid.,* 16, 22; GCS 40, 552.

36. *Ibid.,* 16, 22; GCS 40, 553.

37. *Didascalia apostolorum,* ed. R. H. Connolly, Oxford 1969, 89.

38. Cf. A. Vilela, *La condition collégiale des prêtres au IIIe siècle* (ThH 14),
Paris 1971.

39. SCh 11(2), 66.

40. *Ep.* 3, 3: "Meminisse autem diaconi debent quoniam apostolos id est
episcopos et praepositos Dominus elegit, diaconos autem post ascensum
Domini in caelos apostoli sibi constituerunt episcopatus sui et ecclesiae
ministros. Quod si nos aliquid audere contra Deum possumus qui episcopos
facit, possunt et contra nos audere diaconi a quibus fiunt."

41. *Ep.* 15, 2; 16, 3.

42. *Ep.* 34, 1; E 5, 2.

43. *Ep.* 15, 1; 43, 1.

44. *Ep.* 52, 1.

45. CA II 26, 4.5.6; SCh 320, 239–241.

46. *Ibid.* 30, 1–2; SCh 320, 249–251.

47. *Ibid.* 44, 4; SCh 285.

48. CA VIII 18, 3; SCh 336, 221.

49. *Sacramentarium Serapionis,* in: *Didascalia et Constitutiones Apostolorum,*
ed. F. X. Funk, vol. II: Testimonia et Scripturae propinquae, Paderbornae

1905, 188. The quotation is given here in the Latin translation of the editor. The same use of the word (*constituat*) is found in can. III (XXXIII) of *Constitutiones Ecclesiae Aegypciacae*, De diaconis, *ibidem* 103–104.

50. *Sacramentarium Veronense*, ed. L. C. Mohlberg, Rome 1966, 120–121.

51. *Le Sacramentaire Grégorien I*, ed. J. Deshuesses, Fribourg (Switzerland) 1992, 96–97.

52. Jerome, *Ep.* 146, 1; PL 22, 1192–95: "Audio quemdam in tantam erupisse vecordiam, ut diaconos, presbyteris, id est episcopis anteferret. Nam cum Apostolus perspicue doceat eosdem esse presbyteros, quos episcopos, quid patitur mensarum et viduarum minister, ut super eos se tumidus efferat, ad quorum preces Christi corpus sanguinisque conficitur?" Id., *Comm. in Ez.* VI, cap. 17, 5–6; PL 25; 183B: "Quod multos facere conspicimus, clientes et pauperes, et agricolas, ut taceam de militantium et iudicum violentia, qui opprimunt per potentiam, vel furta committunt, ut de multis parva pauperibus tribuant, et in suis sceleribus glorientur, publiceque diaconus, in Ecclesiis recitet offerentium nomina. Tantum offert illa, tantum ille pollicitus est, placentque sibi ad plausum populi, torquente eis conscientia."

53. *De Trinitate* 1, 27; PG 28; 1157 B: "episkopos, presbyteros, diakonoi homoousioi eisin."

54. Origen, *Hom. in Jer.* 11, 3; *Concilium Ancyranum* can. 14.

55. *Hom 14, 3 in Act.;* PG 60, 116: "Quam ergo dignitatem habuerunt illi (sc. the deacons and the bishops) . . . Atqui haec in Ecclesiis non erat; sed presbyterorum erat oeconomia. Atqui nullus adhuc episcopus erat, praeterquam apostoli tantum. Unde puto nec diaconorum nec presbyterorum tunc fuisse nomen admissum nec manifestum . . ."

56. "And rightly so; for it is not a man, nor an angel, nor an archangel, nor any other created power, but the Paraclete himself who instituted this order, persuading men who are still in the flesh to imitate the service of the angels." *De Sacerdotio* III 4, 1–8; SCh 272, 142.

57. "Graecum codicem legite, et diaconum invenietis. Quod enim interpretatus est latinus, Minister; graecus habet, Diaconus; quia vere diaconus graece, minister latine; quomodo martyr graece, testis latine; apostolus graece, missus latine. Sed iam consuevimus nominibus graecis uti pro latinis. Nam multi codices Evangeliorum sic habent: 'Ubi sum ego, illic et diaconus meus'." *Sermo CCCXXIX, De Stephano martyre VI*, cap. III; PL 38; 1441.

58. *Traditio Apostolica* 10; SCh 11(2), 67.

59. Cf. Tertullian, *To his wife*, 1, 7, 4; SCh 273; *Exhortation to chastity* 13, 4; SCh 319.

60. "It is at the Eastern limits of the Roman Empire that deaconesses finally make their appearance. The first document to refer to them, which is in some sort their birth certificate, is the *Didascalia Apostolorum* . . . known since the publication in 1854 . . . of its Syriac text . . ." A. G. Martimort, *Les diaconesses. Essai historique,* Rome 1982, 31.

61. The most ample collection of all the testimony about this ecclesiastical ministry, accompanied by a theological interpretation, is that of John Pinius, *De diaconissarum ordinatione,* in *Acta Sanctorum,* Sept. 1, Antwerp, 1746, I–XXVII. Most of the Greek and Latin documents referred to by Pinius are reproduced by J. Mayer, *Monumenta de viduis diaconissis virginibusque tractantia,* Bonn 1938. Cf. R. Gryson, *Le ministère des femmes dans l'Église ancienne* (Recherches et synthèses), Gembloux 1972.

62. This norm is repeated in the *Constitutiones Apostolorum* III 19, 1. On the origins of the professionalisation of the clergy, cf. G. Schöllgen, *Die Anfänge der Professionalisierung des Klerus und das Kirchliche Amt in der Syrischen Didaskalie* (JAC. Erg.-Bd. 26), Münster 1998.

63. The compiler was attentive to the nuances of vocabulary. At CA II 11, 3 he says, "we do not allow the priests to ordain (*cheirotonein*) deacons, deaconesses, lectors, servants, cantors or door-keepers: that belongs to the bishops alone." However, he reserves the term *cheirotonia* to the ordination of bishops, priests, deacons and sub-deacons (VIII 4–5; 16–17; 21). He employs the expression *epitithenai tèn (tas) cheira(s)* for deaconesses and lectors (VIII 16, 2; 17, 2). He does not seem to wish to give these expressions a different meaning, since all these impositions of hands are accompanied by an epiclesis of the Holy Spirit. For confessors, virgins, widows, and exorcists, he specifies that there is no *cheirotonia* (VIII 23–26). The compiler additionally distinguishes between *cheirotonia* and *cheirothesia,* which is simply a gesture of blessing (cf. VIII 16, 3 and VIII 28, 2–3). *Cheirothesia* may be practiced by priests in the baptismal rite, the re-integration of penitents, or the blessing of catechumens (cf. II 32, 3; II 18, 7; VII 39, 4).

64. Cf. CA III 20, 2; VIII 16, 5; VIII 28, 4; VIII 46, 10–11.

65. Can. 19 of the Council of Nicaea (325) could be interpreted not as refusing the imposition of hands to all deaconesses in general, but as the simple statement that the deaconesses from the party of Paul of Samosata did not receive the imposition of hands, and "were anyway counted among the laity," and that it was also necessary to re-ordain them, after having re-baptized them, like the other ministers of this dissident group who returned to the Catholic Church. Cf. G. Alberigo, *Les Conciles oecuméniques, Les Décrets,* vol. II, 1, Paris 1994, 54.

66. *Constitutiones Apostolorum,* VIII, 20, 1–2; SCh 336; Metzger, 221–223.

67. Epiphanius of Salamis, *Panarion haer.* 79, 3, 6, ed. K. Holl, GCS 37, 1933, p. 478.

68. Cf. G. Alberigo, *Les Conciles úcuméniques, Les Décrets,* vol. II, 1, Paris 1994, 214.

69. Gregory of Nyssa, *Life of Saint Macrina* 29, 1; SCh 178; Maraval, 236–237.

70. Byzantine Ritual of ordination of deaconesses: *Euchologe du manuscrit grec Barberini* 336, in: Vatican Library, ff 169R-17/v. Quoted by J.-M. Aubert, *Des femmes diacres* (Le Point Théologique 47), Paris 1987, 118–119.

71. Cf. can. 100 (Munier 99). In addition, it is expressly forbidden to women, "even well-instructed and holy" ones, to teach men and to baptize (cf. can. 37. 41; ibidem, 86).

72. Council of Nîmes (394–6), can. 2. Cf. J. Gaudemet, *Conciles gaulois du IV e siècle* (SCh 241), Paris 1977, 127–129.

73. Council of Orange 1 (441), can. 26.

74. Cf. ed. H. I. Vogels, CSEL 81/3, Vienna 1969, 268.

75. Council of Epaone (517), can. 21 (C. de CLERCQ, *Concilia Galliae 511–695,* CCL 148A, 1963, 29). Blessings of women as deaconesses had become widespread because the ritual did not provide a blessing for widows, as was noted in the second Council of Tours (567), can. 21 (*ibidem,* 187).

76. *Ibidem,* 101.

77. Cf. II Council of Tours, can. 20 (*ibidem,* 184).

78. Many commentators have followed the model of *Ambrosiaster* in his Commentary on 1 Timothy 3:11 (CSEL 81, 3; G. L. Muller (Ed.), *Der Empfänger des Weihesakraments. Quellen zur Lehre und Praxis der Kirche, nur Männern das Weihesakrament zu spenden,* Würzburg 1999, 89): "But the Cataphrygians, seizing this opportunity of falling into error, uphold in their foolish rashness, under the pretext that Paul addressed women after deacons, that it is also necessary to ordain deaconesses. They know however that the apostles chose seven deacons (cf. Acts of the Apostles 6:1–6); is it to be supposed that no woman was found suitable at that point, when we read that there were holy women grouped around the eleven apostles (cf. Acts of the Apostles 1:14)? (. . .) And Paul orders women to keep silence in church (cf. 1 Corinthians 14:34–35)." See also John Chrysostom, *In 1 Tim hom.* 11; PG 62, 555; Epiphanius, *Haer.* 79, 3 (G. L. Müller, *Quellen,* 88); *Council of Orange* (G. L. Müller, *Quellen,* 98); Council of Dovin (Armenia, 527): "Feminis non licet ministeria diaconissae praestare nisi ministerium baptismi" (G. L. Müller, *Quellen,* 105); Isidore of Seville, *De Eccl. Off.* II, 18, 11 (G. L. Müller, *Quellen,* 109); *Decretum Gratiani,* can. 15 (G. L. Müller, *Quellen,* 115); Magister Rufinus, *Summa Decretorum,* can. 27, q. 1 (G. L. Müller, *Quellen,*

320); Robert of Yorkshire, *Liber poenitentialis*, q. 6, 42 (G. L. Müller, *Quellen*, 322); Thomas Aquinas, *In 1 Timothy* III, 11 (G. L. Müller, *Quellen*, 333); etc.

79. Cf. Vanzan, *Le Diaconat permanent féminin. Ombres et lumières*, in: Documentation Catholique 2203 (1999) 440–446. The author refers to the discussions which have taken place between R. Gryson, A. G. Martimort, C. Vagaggini and C. Marucci. Cf. L. Scheffczyk (ed.), *Diakonat und Diakonissen*, St. Ottilien 2002, especially M. Hauke, *Die Geschichte der Diakonissen. Nachwort und Literaturnachtrag zur Neuauflage des Standardwerkes von Martimort über die Diakonissen*, pp. 321–376.

Chapter 3

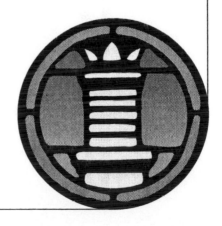

The Disappearance of the Permanent Diaconate

I. THE CHANGES IN THE DIACONAL MINISTRY

At Rome, from the third century onward, each deacon was at the head of one of the seven pastoral regions, while the priests had a smaller *titulus* (the future parish). Deacons were charged with administering funds and organizing charitable works. The Council of Neo-Caesarea, at the beginning of the fourth century, had asked that each Church, however big it was, should have no more than seven deacons, in memory of Acts of the Apostles 6:1–6.[80] This provision, still remembered by Isidore of Seville[81] but infrequently observed, particularly in the East,[82] heightened the prestige of the diaconal order and encouraged deacons still more to leave their original functions to other members of the clergy. They were to define themselves more and more explicitly by reference to their liturgical attributes, and come into conflict with the priests.

The functions of deacons were progressively being taken over by other ministers. As early as the *Traditio Apostolica* (13), "subdeacons" were appointed "to follow the deacon." Those who "followed the deacon" soon became his "acolytes."[83] The acolytes had the job of taking the *fermentum*, the portion of the bishop's Eucharist, to the priests of the *tituli* in the town. It was also the acolytes who took it to those who were absent. The "door-keepers" also fulfilled a function which had originally been the task of the deacons. It may be considered that the minor ministries resulted from a sharing-out of diaconal functions.

The state of subdeacon approached that of deacon more closely. Toward 400, in the East, the Council of Laodicea tried to prevent sub-deacons from encroaching on the liturgical functions of deacons, stating that they should content themselves with looking after the doors.[84] Subdeacons adopted the rule of life of deacons.

The African councils of the last part of the fourth century demanded continence on the part of clergy "who serve at the altar."[85] *The Canones in causa Apiarii* (419–425) extended this requirement to subdeacons, "who touch the sacred mysteries."[86] Leo the Great (440–461) confirmed this requirement for sub-deacons.[87] Leo made a ready distinction between *sacerdotes* (the bishop and priests), *levitae* (the deacons and subdeacons), and *clerici* (the other ministers).[88]

Cyprian had already found it necessary to remind people that deacons had been instituted by the apostles and not by the Lord himself.[89] In certain places deacons must have been tempted to take the place of priests. The Council of Arles (314) reminded them that they could not offer the Eucharist (can. 15) and that they should show due honor to priests (can. 18). Nicaea forbade them to give communion to priests, or to receive it before the bishops: they were to receive communion from the bishop or from a priest, and after them. They were not to sit among the priests. "Let the deacons remain within the limits of their competence, knowing that they are the servants of the bishop and are inferior to priests in rank" (can. 19).[90]

Toward 378 the anonymous *Ambrosiaster*, composed at Rome, witnessed to the persistent tension between the presbyterate and the diaconate.[91] Jerome went further, exclaiming that deacons were not superior to priests![92] Priests came to exercise more and more of the functions reserved to deacons, at the same time as they received progressively more autonomy in their responsibilities within the urban *tituli* and the rural parishes. Deacons, who had wanted to exercise the liturgical and teaching functions reserved to priests, now suffered from a backlash against such an attitude: they became subordinate to the priests, their direct link with the bishop faded away, and they ended up having no specific function. The clergy of the Church in the Empire progressively forgot about their function of service and maintained the concept of the sacredness of the priesthood, toward which all the other degrees of the clerical career tended. The deacons were the first to suffer the consequences of this.

Toward the end of the fifth century the thinking of Pseudo-Dionysius began to have a lasting influence both in the East and in the West. In Dionysius's hierarchically structured view of heaven and the Church, every being received its specific determination and function from the order to which it belonged. The ecclesiastical hierarchy was composed of two groups of three. The first group contained the order of the hierarchs or bishops, the order of priests, and the order of "liturges" or ministers. This latter order included the ecclesiastical orders from deacon to door-keeper. The diaconate no longer had any specific mark to distinguish it from the other orders beneath the priests.[93]

Still toward the end of the fifth century, the career path of the clergy was defined in function of their liturgical attributes as well as the demand of continence for those who served in the sanctuary or related positions. Leo the Great considered that the ideal path, before proceeding to the priesthood and the episcopate, was to go through all the degrees of the clergy with an appropriate interval between each.[94] The number and names of the different degrees (*gradus*) of the clergy fluctuated. There were eight at Rome in the time of Pope Cornelius.[95] In the fifth century, the door-keeper and the exorcist were no longer included among them.[96] The author of *De septem ordinibus* at the beginning of the fifth century speaks of grave-diggers, door-keepers, lectors, subdeacons, deacons, priests and bishops.[97] The *Statuta Ecclesiae antiqua*, also composed in the south of Gaul toward 480, re-proposed a list of eight *officiales ecclesiae* who received an *ordinatio*. bishop, priest and deacon received an imposition of hands, the candidates for orders inferior to these (subdeacon, acolyte, exorcist, lector and door-keeper) were installed by a rite of handing over of the instruments of their office.[98] Thus the functions which had in the past been autonomous and practical, became stages in the career path toward the priesthood. The sacramentary of Verona (around 560–580) contained a prayer of "consecration" for the bishop and the priest, and a prayer of "blessing" for the deacon. It said that the deacon was essentially ordained in view of liturgical ministry; he should be an example of chastity.[99]

Progress through the clerical career path was still often made *per saltum*. At Rome in the ninth century the sub-diaconate was the only obligatory degree before major orders. All the popes between 687 and 891 had been subdeacons. Five had then become deacons before being raised to the episcopate, and nine passed directly from the subdiaconate to the priesthood and then to the episcopate.

One of the former competencies of deacons, the management of the funds of the community, was also lost to them. The Council of Chalcedon (451) sanctioned this development, laying down that each bishop should entrust this responsibility to an officer chosen from "among his own clergy" (can. 26), not necessarily from among the deacons. Aid to the poor was often looked after by monasteries. Under Gregory the Great, the huge "Patrimony of Saint Peter" was managed by *defensores* or *notarii*, who were added to the clergy, in other words at least given the tonsure.

In the East, the Byzantine Council *In Trullo* in 692 analyzed the contents of Acts of the Apostles 6:1–6. The Seven, it observed, were neither deacons nor priests nor bishops. They were people who were "charged with administering the common property of the community of that time . . . They are an example of charity" (can. 7).[100] At the end of the ninth century in the East, the deacons still formed a permanent order of clergy, but for liturgical needs alone. The Byzantine rite had two preparatory stages for the sacred ministry: those of lector (or cantor) and subdeacon, conferred by *cheirothesia*, and obligatory before the diaconate.[101] But the subdiaconate was often conferred at the same time as the lectorate, or just before the diaconate. According to the ritual of the *Constitutiones Apostolorum*, which was still applied in the East, admission to the minor orders of subdiaconate and lectorate was accomplished by the imposition of hands and the handing-over of the instruments of office. In the West too, the activity of deacons was reduced, in practice, to their liturgical functions.[102] When rural parishes were created, the Councils insisted that they should be endowed with a priest. It did not occur to them to call for deacons.[103]

From the tenth century onward, at least in the Holy Roman Empire, the rule was ordination *per gradum*. The reference document was the *Pontifical Romano-Germanique*,[104] composed at Mainz around 950. It was in direct continuity with the tradition of the *Ordines Romani* of the preceding centuries,[105] to which it added plentiful elements from the Germanic ritual. The ordination of deacons included the handing-over of the book of the Gospels, signifying their function of proclaiming the Gospel in the liturgy. The deacon here appears closer to the subdeacon than to the priest. The priest was the man of the Eucharist; the deacon attended him at the altar. This ritual was introduced at Rome through the Germanic emperors' zeal for reform at the end of the tenth century. Rome fell into line with the *per gradum* career path for clergy which was the rule in the Empire. From that time on the history of the ordination rites attests perfect continuity.[106] The First Lateran Council (1123) can. 7, and the Second Lateran Council (1139) can. 6, deprived of their office any clergy who contracted marriage, from the subdiaconate inclusive. Can. 7 of the

Second Lateran Council declared that such a marriage would be null and void.[107] From that time on the Latin Church normally ordained only celibate men.

The patristic and liturgical texts of the first millennium all mentioned the ordination of bishops, priests, and deacons, but they did not yet explicitly raise the question of the sacramentality of each of these ordinations.

The history of the ministries shows that the priesthood has had a tendency to take over the functions of the lesser orders. When the progression through the various orders became stabilized, each grade possessed the competencies of the previous grade plus some additional ones—what a deacon can do, a priest can also do. The bishop, being at the summit of the hierarchy, can exercise all the ecclesiastical functions. The fact that the different competencies fitted together in this way and that lesser functions were taken over by higher ones, the fragmentation of the original role of deacons into many different functions to be performed by subordinate clergy, and the progression to the higher functions *per gradum*, all go to explain how the diaconate as a permanent ministry lost its reason for existing. All that was left were liturgical tasks exercised for a given time by candidates for the priesthood.

II. TOWARD THE DISAPPEARANCE OF DEACONESSES

After the tenth century deaconesses were only named in connection with charitable institutions. A Jacobite author of that time notes: "In ancient times, deaconesses were ordained. Their function was to look after women so that they should not have to uncover themselves before the bishop. But when religion spread more widely and it was decided to administer Baptism to infants, this function was abolished."[108] We find the same statement in the Pontifical of Patriarch Michael of Antioch (1166–1199).[109] When commenting on can. 15 of the Council of Chalcedon, Theodore Balsamon, at the end of the twelfth century, observed that "the topic of this canon has altogether fallen into disuse. For today deaconesses are no longer ordained, although the name of deaconesses is wrongly given to those who belong to communities of ascetics . . ."[110] Deaconesses had become nuns. They lived in monasteries which no longer practiced works of *diakonia* except in the field of education, medical care, or parish service.

The presence of deaconesses is still attested in Rome at the end of the eighth century. While the Roman rituals had previously not mentioned deaconesses, the sacramentary *Hadrianum,* sent by the pope to Charlemagne and spread by him throughout the Frankish world, includes an *Oratio ad diaconam faciendam.* It was in fact a blessing, placed as an appendix among other rites of first institution. The Carolingian texts often combined deaconesses and abbesses. The Council of Paris of 829 contained a general prohibition on women performing any liturgical function.[111] The Decretals of Pseudo-Isidore contain no mention of deaconesses, and neither does a Bavarian Pontifical from the first half of the ninth century.[112] A century later, in the Pontifical Romano-Germanique of Mainz, the prayer *Ad diaconam faciendam* is to be found after the *ordinatio abbatissae,* between the *consecratio virginum* and the *consecratio viduarum.* Once again, this was merely a blessing accompanied by the handing-over of the stole and veil by the bishop, as well as the nuptial ring and the crown. Like widows, the deaconess promised continence. This is the last mention of "deaconesses" found in the Latin rituals. In fact the Pontifical of Guillaume Durand at the end of the thirteenth century speaks of deaconesses only with reference to the past.[113]

In the Middle Ages, the nursing and teaching religious orders of nuns fulfilled in practice the functions of *diakonia* without, however, being ordained for this ministry. The title, with no corresponding ministry, was given to women who were instituted as widows or abbesses. Right up until the thirteenth century, Abbesses were sometimes called deaconesses.

---

80. Council of Neo-Caesarea (314 or 319), can. 15, in: Mansi, *Sacrorum conciliorum nova et amplissima collectio,* vol. 2, Paris-Leipzig, 1901 (new edition), 539.

81. Isidore of Seville, *De Ecclesiasticis Officiis,* 2, 8.

82. There were one hundred deacons at Constantinople in the time of Justinian. Cf. Justinian, *Novellae* III, 1 (*Corpus Juris civilis,* ed. Kriegel, vol. III, Leipzig 1887, 20).

83. Cf. *Constitutiones Apostolorum* II, 28, 6.

84. Cf. can. 21.22.43, in P.-Joannou, *Discipline générale antique 11e–IXe siècle,* 1–2, Rome 1962, 139–148.

85. Council of Carthage sub Genethlio (390), can. 2, in C. Munier, *Concilia Africae,* CCSL 259, Turnhout 1974, 13.

86. Cf. can. 25, *ibidem* 108–109.

87. Leo the Great, *Ep.* 14, 4 to Anastasius of Thessalonica; PL 54, 672–673.

88. Leo the Great, *Ep.* 14, 4.

89. Cf. chapter II *supra,* note 40.

90. Cf. G. Alberigo, *Les Conciles oecuméniques, Les Décrets,* vol. II, 1, Paris 1994, 54.

91. The short treatise *De jactantia Romanorum diaconum* (CSEL 50, 193–198) reproves deacons for wanting to work their way up into the ranks of the priests, for refusing tasks of service, and for concerning themselves with liturgical singing alone.

92. Jerome, *Letter 146 to Evangelus;* PL 22, 1192–1195.

93. Pseudo-Dionysius, *Ecclesiastical Hierarchy* V, 7; V, 6; PG 3, 506–508.

94. Leo the Great, *Ep.* 6, 6 to Anastasius of Thessalonica; PL 54, 620. Leo himself was a deacon when he was elected to the episcopate. See also L. Duchesne, *Liber Pontificalis* I, de Boccard, Paris 1981, 238–239.

95. Cf. Eusebius of Caesarea, *Hist. Eccl.* VI, 43.

96. Cf. *The Decretals of Siricius,* PL 13, 1142–1143; *The Decretals of Innocent I,* PL 20, 604–605.

97. Pseudo-Jerome, *Ep. XII de septem ordinibus ecclesiae,* PL 30, 150–162.

98. Cf. C. Munier, Les *Statuta Ecclesiae antiqua,* Editions-études critiques, Paris 1960, 95–99. The author adds the psalmist to this list. Isidore of Seville, *Etymologies* VII, 12, PL 82, 290 spoke of nine degrees, including the psalmist. In his terminology, all nine *ordines* were also called *sacramenta,* cf. *De Ecclesiasticis Officiis* 2, 21.

99. Cf. L. C. Mohlberg, *Sacramentarium Veronense* (RED. F I), Rome 1956, 120–121.

100. P.-Joannou, *Discipline générale antique IIe–IXe siècle. Les canons des conciles oecuméniques,* I, 1, 132–134.

101. Cf. F. Mercenier and F. Paris, *La Prière des Eglises de rite byzantin,* 2 vols, Prieuré d'Ainay sur Meuse 1937. From the eighth century onward, usage became fixed. The term *cheirotonia* was now reserved to the ordinations of bishops, priests and deacons; while *cheirothesia* was the term used for orders below those. Thus can. 15 of the Second Council of Nicaea (ed. G. Alberigo, vol. II/I, 149). Cf. C. Vogel, *Chirotonie et chirothésie* in: Irénikon 37 (1972) 7–21; 207–238.

102. Pseudo-Jerome, *De septem ordinibus,* says that deacons "do not leave the temple of the Lord . . . They are the altar of Christ . . . Without the deacon, the priest has no name nor origin nor function" (PL 30, 153).

103. Cf. Council of Aix-la-Chapelle 817, can. 11 (C. J. Hefele -H. Leclercq, *Histoire des Conciles,* vol. IV, Paris, 1910, 27).

104. C. Vogel, *Le Pontifical romano-germanique du dixième siècle,* 3 vols. (Studi e testi 226–227–269), Vatican 1963–1972.

105. See M. Andrieu, *Les Ordines Romani du haut moyen âge* (SSL 24), Louvain 1951.

106. The various Roman Pontificals of the twelfth century had as their common foundation the tenth-century *Pontifical Romano-Germanique.* Cf. M. Andrieu, *Le Pontifical romain au moyen âge,* vol. I *Le Pontifical du XIIe siècle* (Studi e testi 86), Vatican 1938. This was widely used in the Latin Church and was brought up to date by Innocent III. See M. Andrieu, *Ibidem,* vol. II *Le Pontifical de la Curie romaine du XIIIe siècle* (Studi e testi 87), Vatican 1940. This in its turn was included in the Pontifical composed by Guillaume Durand, bishop of Mende at the end of the thirteenth century. Cf. M. Andrieu, *Ibidem,* vol. III *Le Pontifical de Guillaume Durand* (Studi e testi 88), Vatican 1940. It was to serve as a model for the edition printed by Burchard of Strasbourg in 1485.

107. Cf. G. Alberigo, *op. cit.,* vol. II/1, 419 and 435.

108. Cf. G. Khouri-Sarkis, *Le livre du guide de Yahya ibn Jarîr,* in: Orient syrien 12 (1967), 303–318.

109. "Long ago the *cheirotonia* or ordination was also done for deaconesses: and for that reason the rite concerning them was given in ancient manuscripts. In those times deaconesses were needed mainly for the Baptism of women . . ." (quoted by A. G. Martimort, *Les diaconesses,* 167).

110. *Scholia in concilium Chalcedonense;* PG 137, 441 (quoted by A. G. Martimort, *Les diaconesses,* 171).

111. Cap. 45 (ed. A Werminghoff, *Concilia aevi Karolini,* vol. I, 639).

112. Cf. F. Unterkircher, *Das Kollectar-Pontifikale des Bischofs Baturich von Regensburg (817–848),* Spicilegium Friburgense 8, Freiburg 1962.

113. Between *De ordinatione abbatissae* and *De benedictione et consecratione virginum,* the passage *De ordinatione diaconissae* occupies a few lines phrased as follows: "Diaconissa olim, non tamen ante annum quadragesimum, ordinabatur hoc modo . . ." See M. Andrieu, *op. cit.,* vol. III (Lib. I, XXI–XXIII) 411.

Chapter 4

The Sacramentality of the Diaconate from the Twelfth to the Twentieth Centuries

The sacramentality of the diaconate is a question that remains *implicit* in biblical, patristic, and liturgical texts that have just been discussed. We now need to see how the Church first became *explicitly* conscious of it in a period in which, apart from certain rare exceptions, the diaconate was simply a stage on the way to the priesthood.

I. In the First Scholastic Teaching

Although "sacramentality" can have a broad, generic meaning, in the strict sense it refers to the seven sacraments (outward and effective signs of grace), among which is the sacrament of "Holy Orders." Within this sacrament were different "orders" or "grades," between seven and nine in number. The diaconate and the priesthood were always listed among the *ordines sacri* of the sacrament, and the subdiaconate began to be included among them because of its requirement of celibacy; the episcopate was excluded from them in most cases.[114]

According to Peter Lombard (†1160),[115] the diaconate was an *ordo* or *gradus officiorum* (the sixth). Although he held that all the *ordines* were *spirituales et sacri*, he underlined the excellence of the diaconate and the priesthood, the only ones that existed in the primitive Church by the will of the apostles, while the others had been instituted by the Church in the course of time. He did not consider the episcopate to share in this excellence, saying that it did not belong to the sacramental *ordines* but rather to the domain of dignities and offices.[116]

II. From Saint Thomas Aquinas (†1273) to Trent (1563)

1. Affirmation of sacramentality

Saint Thomas's teaching on the diaconate[117] included the fact that it was a sacrament insofar as it belonged to Holy Orders, one of the seven sacraments of the new law. He considered that each of the different orders constituted in some way a sacramental reality; however, only three (priest, deacon and subdeacon) could strictly be said to be *ordines sacri* by reason of their special relation to the Eucharist.[118] But it should not be concluded that their sacramentality meant that the priesthood and the diaconate were different sacraments; the distinction between the orders did not indicate that each was a universal or integral whole, but indicated a potestative wholeness.[119]

The way that the unity and oneness of the sacrament of Holy Orders was bound together in its different grades had to do with their reference to the Eucharist, *Sacramentum sacramentorum*.[120] Because of that, the different orders needed a sacramental consecration depending on their type of power with respect to the Eucharist. Through ordination priests received the power to consecrate, while deacons received the power to serve the priests in the administration of the sacraments.[121]

The relationship of each order to the Eucharist became the deciding factor in avoiding the idea that each order gave the power to administer a specific sacrament. The same criterion also served to exclude the orders of psalmist and cantor from the sacramental orders. But this criterion was also used to exclude the episcopate from sacramentality.[122] In spite of everything, although Saint Thomas refuses to recognize in the episcopate any sort of power superior to that of the priest in relation to the *verum corpus Christi*, he considers the episcopate to be also an *ordo* in a certain way, by reason of the powers that the bishop holds over the *corpus mysticum*.[123]

Because the diaconate is a sacrament, it is an *ordo* which imprints a character on the soul. Saint Thomas applies this doctrine to Baptism, Confirmation, and Holy Orders. His thinking on this developed with time. Starting from the priesthood of Christ he defined

Holy Orders alone as imprinting a character (*In IV Sent.*), but finally defined the complete doctrine of character (*STh.*).[124]

On the subject of the diaconate, he explained all its *potestates*, in relation to the *dispensatio* of the sacraments, as something that seemed to belong rather within the domain of what was "licit" and not within the domain of a new radical enablement with regard to the "validity" of the functions in question.[125] In his turn, in *STh* III q67 a1, he asks whether evangelizing and baptizing are part of the deacon's office, and he answers that no direct administration of the sacraments belongs to the diaconate *quasi ex proprio officio*, any more than any task in relation with *docere*, but only with *cathechizare*.[126]

2. Sacramentality called into question

Durandus of Saint-Pourçain (†1334) represented a doctrinal line that was to reappear intermittently up until the present day. According to this line, only ordination to the priesthood is a "sacrament"; the other orders, including the diaconate, were only "sacramentals."[127] The reasons for his position were as follows:

a) with regard to the Eucharist, the distinction between the power of consecrating, which belonged exclusively to the order of the priesthood (which should be considered a sacrament) and the preparatory actions, which belonged to the other orders (merely considered as sacramentals);

b) in the same way as with Baptism, there was a "potestas ad suscipiendum sacramenta"; but it was only the priesthood that was granted a "postestas ordinis ad conficiendum vel conferendum ea," which was not granted to any of the orders inferior to the priesthood, not even to the diaconate;

c) ordination to the priesthood grants a power *ad posse* and not *ad licere*, so that the ordained priest can really do something that he could not do before his ordination. The diaconate, on the other hand, grants the capacity to do *licite* something that he could in fact do before, although illicitly, and this is why the diaconate can be considered as an institution or ecclesial deputation to exercise certain functions;

d) it is also demanded by the unity of the sacrament of Orders and the evaluation of the priesthood as the fullness of this sacrament, since otherwise it would be hard to preserve the meaning of what

Saint Thomas said on the unity and oneness of the Sacrament
of Holy Orders;[128]

e) the distinction between *sacramentum* and *sacramentalia* did
not, however, prevent Durandus from saying that each of the orders
imprints a "character." He distinguished in his turn between a *deputatio*
which had its origin in God himself, and made the order in question
a *sacramentum,* and an ecclesiastical *deputatio* instituted by the Church,
which only made the orders in question (all the other orders)
sacramentalia. In this sense it could be said that the diaconate imprints
a character; the doubt or debate concerned exactly when the character
was imprinted, since some maintained that it would come "in
traditione libri evangeliorum" (an opinion which Durandus rejected)
while others held that it came "in impositione manuum" (an opinion
which he appeared to adopt).[129]

3. The Teaching of Trent (1563)

The Council of Trent chose to make a dogmatic definition of Holy
Orders as a sacrament; the direction of its doctrinal statements leaves
no doubt on the subject. However, it is not clear to what extent the
sacramentality of the diaconate should be considered as being included
in this definition. The question has remained a controversial one to the
present day, although very few people indeed now debate the subject.
This makes it necessary to interpret the statements of the Council
of Trent.

As against the denials of the Reformers, Trent declared
the existence of a *hierarchia in Ecclesia ordinatione divina* (which led
to a rejection of the statement "omnes christianos promiscue Novi
Testamenti sacerdotes esse") and also a *hierarchia ecclesiastica* (which
led to the distinction between the different grades within the
sacrament of Holy Orders).[130]

The references by Trent to the diaconate (which it also refers
to explicitly) need to be set within the general theology of the sacrament
of Holy Orders. However, it is not entirely certain that the dogmatic
declarations of Trent on the sacramentality and the sacramental
character of the priesthood, to which Trent refers explicitly, include an
intention on the part of the Council to define the sacramentality of
the diaconate as well.

According to Trent, deacons are mentioned directly in the NT, although it is not stated that they were instituted directly by Christ the Savior. In accordance with the way the other orders are envisaged, the diaconate is also conceived of as a help to exercising "dignius et maiore cum veneratione ministerium tam sancti sacerdotii" and to serve the priesthood "ex officio" (it is not said to be "ad ministerium episcopi"). Furthermore, the diaconate appears to be a stage on the way to the priesthood–there is no explicit mention of a permanent diaconate.[131]

When Trent defined dogmatically that *ordo* or *sacra ordination* was "vere sacramentum,"[132] there was no explicit mention of the diaconate, which was included among the *ordines ministrorum*.[133] Thus, if the dogmatic statement of sacramentality is to be applied to the diaconate, it should perhaps be applied equally to the other *ordines ministrorum*, which seems excessive and unjustified.

Something similar can be said on the subject of the doctrine of "sacramental character."[134] In view of the expressions used by the Council, there can be no doubt that Trent referred explicitly and directly to the "priests of the NT," to distinguish them clearly from the "laypeople." There is no mention made of "deacons," either direct or indirect; therefore it would be difficult to see in the text of Trent any intention to establish the dogma of character for the diaconate.

Can. 6 merits particular attention ("si quis dixerit in Ecclesia catholica non esse hierarchiam, divina ordinatione institutam, quae constat ex episcopis, presbyteris et ministris, a.s."[135]) because of different interpretations of the word *ministris:* deacons, or deacons and other ministers, or all the other orders? Right up until the day before its approval (14. 7. 1563), the text of can. 6 said "et aliis ministris." That day, in view of petitions made by a Spanish group, the expression *aliis ministris* was altered to exclude the word *aliis*. But the reasons and scope of this change are not very clear.[136]

How should the term *ministris*, and their inclusion in the *hierarchia*, be interpreted? The exclusion of the word *aliis* means, according to some, that the dividing line within the ecclesiastical hierarchy should be drawn between *sacerdotes* (bishops and priests) on the one hand, and *ministri* on the other; the suppression of the word *aliis* was intended to stress once again that the bishops and priests are not "nudi ministri" but "sacerdotes Novi Testamenti." The history of the text in question, in the light of its previous formulations, would seem to suggest a broad understanding of *ministri,* to include "diaconos caeterosque ministros," corresponding to a triple division of the hierarchy ("praecipue episcopi, deinde praesbyteri, diaconi et alii ministri"). But it must not be forgotten that according to other authors the suppression of the term *aliis* meant that the subdiaconate and other minor orders were excluded from the hierarchy "divina ordinatione instituta"—an expression whose interpretation is in its turn polemical.[137]

To sum up, whether one interprets it exclusively or inclusively, it cannot be doubted that deacons are included in the term *ministri.* But the dogmatic consequences concerning their sacramentality and their inclusion in the hierarchy will differ, depending on whether the word *ministri* refers to deacons alone, or includes the other orders too.

III. THEOLOGICAL NUANCES AFTER TRENT

After the Council of Trent, in the theology of the sixteenth and seventeenth centuries, a majority of opinions maintained the sacramentality of the diaconate, with only a minority questioning or denying it. However, the form in which this sacramentality was defended had many differing nuances, and it was generally considered to be a point which had not been dogmatically defined by Trent, and which was reasserted doctrinally in the *Roman Catechism* where it describes the functions of deacons.[138]

Thus for example, F. de Vitoria (†1546) considers as *probabilissima* the opinion that "solum sacramentum est sacerdotium" and that all the other orders are sacramentals. D. de Soto (†1560), for his part, although in favor of the sacramentality of both the diaconate and the subdiaconate, considered that anyone who followed Durandus was not to be reprehended.[139]

Robert Bellarmine (†1621) well described the *status quaestionis* at that point. He established the sacramentality of Holy Orders ("vere ac proprie sacramentum novae legis") as a fundamental principle admitted by all Catholic theologians and denied by (Protestant) heretics. But as regarded the sacramentality of the individual orders he felt it necessary to make a distinction, because although there was unanimous agreement on the sacramentality of the priesthood, this was not the case for the other orders.[140]

Bellarmine declared himself clearly in favor of the sacramentality of the episcopate ("ordinatio episcopalism sacramentum est vere ac proprie dictum"), as against the scholastics of old who denied it; and he considered this an *assertio certissima*, based on Scripture and Tradition. Moreover, he spoke of an episcopal character that was distinct from and superior to the character of the presbyterate.

As regards the doctrine of the sacramentality of the diaconate, Bellarmine adopted it, considering it very probable; however, he did not take it as a certainty *ex fide*, since it could not be deduced from the evidence of Scripture nor Tradition nor any explicit pronouncement on the part of the Church.[141]

Bellarmine was also in favor of the sacramentality of the subdiaconate, basing his opinion on the doctrine of character, on celibacy, and on the common opinion of theologians, although he recognized that this doctrine was not as certain as that of the diaconate.[142] Still less certain, in his view, was the sacramentality of the other minor orders.

IV. THE SACRAMENTALITY OF THE DIACONATE IN VATICAN II

Concerning deacons or the diaconate in the texts of Vatican II (SC 86; LG 20, 28, 29, 41; OE 17; CD 15; DV 25; AG 15, 16) the sacramentality of both modes (permanent and transitory) was taken for granted. Sometimes it was stated simply in passing, or indirectly, or faintly. Taken all together, the texts of Vatican II repeated what had been the majority opinion in theology up to that time, but went no further. Neither did the Council clarify a number of uncertainties that were expressed in the course of the debates.

1. In the conciliar debates

The sacramentality of the diaconate was a theme tackled in several interventions in the second period of the Council (1963). The result was a majority in favor, particularly among those who upheld the institution of the permanent diaconate; among who opposed such an institution, there was no majority in favor of the sacramentality of the diaconate.[143]

In the *relatio* of the doctrinal Commission, some explanatory notes on the text are presented which are of interest in interpreting it. The notes give the exegetical reason for not directly mentioning Acts of the Apostles 6:1–6,[144] and also explain the moderate way in which the sacramentality of the diaconate is mentioned, as caused by unwillingness to give the impression of condemning those who questioned it.[145] The conciliar debate did not in fact reach unanimity on the sacramental nature of the diaconate.

Also of interest for interpretation of the texts are the nuances introduced into the summary of the discussion. Among the arguments in favor of restoration, mention was first made of the sacramental nature of the diaconate, of which the Church ought not to be deprived. Among the arguments against restoration the main one was undoubtedly that of celibacy. But others were added, such as whether or not the diaconate was needed for tasks that could be carried out by laypeople. The following questions were asked under this heading: whether all tasks were to be considered, or only some of them; whether those tasks were of a regular nature or were exceptional; whether or not there was a privation of the special graces linked to the sacramentality of the diaconate; whether negative or positive influences on the apostolate of the laity could be considered; whether it was appropriate to recognize ecclesially, by ordination, the diaconal tasks that were in fact already being carried out; and whether deacons' (and especially married deacons') possible situation as a "bridge" between the higher clergy and the laity could be considered.[146]

2. In the texts of Vatican II

In LG 29, the proposition according to which there was an imposition of hands on deacons *"non ad sacerdotium, sed ad ministerium"* was to become a key reference for the theological understanding of the diaconate. However, many questions have been left open up until the present day for the following reasons: the suppression of the reference to the bishop in the formula which was settled upon;[147] the dissatisfaction felt by certain people about the ambiguity in that formula;[148] the interpretation given by the Commission;[149] and the scope of the actual distinction between *sacerdotium* and *ministerium*.

In LG 28a, the term *ministerium* is used in a double sense in turn: a) to refer to the ministry of the bishops, who as successors of the apostles partake of the "consecration" and "mission" received by Christ from his Father, which they hand on in various degrees to different individuals, without explicit mention being made of deacons;[150] b) to refer to the "ecclesiastical ministry" as a whole, divinely established on different levels, embracing those who from antiquity have been called bishops, priests, and deacons.[151] In the relevant note, Vatican II gives a reference to Trent, session 23, cap. 2 and can. 6.[152] The same sort of caution can be observed in both sources in the expressions that relate to the diversity of grades: "ordinatione divina" (Trent), "divinitus institutum" (Vatican II); "ab ipso Ecclesiae initio" (Trent), "ab antiquo" or else "inde ab Apostolis" according to AG 16 (Vatican II).[153]

The statement that relates most directly to the sacramentality of the diaconate is found in LG 29a: "*gratia enim sacramentali roborati, in diaconia liturgiae, verbi et caritatis populo Dei, in communione cum Episcopo eiusque presbyterio, inserviunt*"; and also in AG 16: "ut ministerium suum per *gratiam sacramentalem* diaconatus efficacius expleant." The expression *gratia sacramentalis* is prudent, appropriate for an interjection, and much more nuanced than the formula "sacramental ordination" employed in the previous project of LG in 1963. Why was this caution apparent in the expressions finally used? The doctrinal Commission referred to the basis in tradition of what is affirmed, and to the concern to avoid giving the impression that those who had doubts on the subject were being condemned.[154]

3. The sacramentality of the diaconate in postconciliar developments

1. Mention must first be made of the document that puts the Council's decisions into effect, i.e. the *Motu Proprio* of Pope Paul VI, *Sacrum diaconatus ordinem* (1967). In what concerns the theological nature of the diaconate, it takes up what Vatican II said about the *gratia* of the diaconate, while adding a reference to the indelible "character" (absent from the Council texts), and it is understood as a "stable" service.[155]

As a grade of the sacrament of Holy Orders, it bestows the capacity to exercise tasks that mostly belong to the domain of the liturgy (eight out of the eleven mentioned). In some expressions, these appear as tasks that are deputized or delegated.[156] Thus it is not clear up to what point the diaconal "character" confers the capacity for some competencies or powers which could only be exercised by reason of previous sacramental ordination; since there is another way of accessing them (by delegation or deputizing, and not by reason of the sacrament of Holy Orders).

2. The most recent step taken in the *Motu Proprio* of Pope Paul VI, *Ad Pascendum* (1972) refers to the instituting of the permanent diaconate (not excluding it as a transitory stage) as a "middle order" between the upper hierarchy and the rest of the People of God. In what concerns sacramentality, as well as considering this *medius ordo* as "signum vel sacramentum ipsius Christi Domini, qui non venit ministrari, sed ministrare," the document presupposes the sacramentality of the diaconate and limits itself to repeating the aforementioned expressions such as *sacra ordination* or *sacrum ordinem*.[157]

3. Following some positions which had already been taken up before Vatican II, certain authors expressed their doubts with regard to the sacramentality of the diaconate more explicitly and with detailed arguments after the Council, too. Their motives were varied. J. Beyer (1980) primarily presented his analysis of the conciliar texts, whose silence on the distinction between the power of "order" and of "jurisdiction" seemed to him to avoid rather than provide a solution to the questions that were still unresolved.[158] The same would apply to the fluctuation in meaning that could be accorded to the term *minister-ium*, and the contrast between it and *sacerdotium*. He further evaluated the caution shown in the Council texts not only as the result of concern to avoid condemning anyone, but also as a result of doctrinal hesitations.[159] This was why further clarification was needed of the question: "estne diaconatus pars sacerdotii sicut et episcopatus atque presbyteratus unum sacerdotium efficiunt?" This need was not satisfied by referring to the "common priesthood" of the faithful and excluding deacons from the "sacrificing" priesthood (cf. Philips). According to Tradition, the ministerial priesthood was "unum" and "unum sacramen-tum." If it was this sacramental priesthood alone which rendered someone capable of acting *in persona Christi* with effect *ex opere operato,* then it would be hard to call the diaconate a "sacrament" because it was not instituted to accomplish any act *in persona Christi* with effect *ex opere operato.*

Additionally, further careful investigation was needed into the statements of Trent and also into the normative value of its references to the diaconate.[160] The acts of Vatican II, the development of the schemas, the various interventions and the *relatio* of the relevant Commission, also needed a careful re-reading. It could be concluded from this *relatio* that a solution had not altogether been found of the difficulties with regard to the following points: a) the exegetical foundation of the institution of the diaconate (Acts of the Apostles 6:1–6 was excluded because it was open to debate, and consideration was limited to the simple mentions of deacons in Philippians 1:1 and 1 Timothy 3:8–12); b) the theological justification of the sacramental nature of the diaconate, in connection with the intention of re-establishing its permanent mode.

In conclusion: if Vatican II spoke cautiously and *ex obliquo* of the sacramental nature of the diaconate, it was not only from a concern not to condemn anyone, but rather because of the "incertitudo doctrinae."[161] Therefore, to confirm its sacramental nature, neither the majority opinion of theologians (which had also existed concerning the subdiaconate), nor the mere description of the rite of ordination (which needed to be clarified from other sources) nor the mere imposition of hands (which could be nonsacramental in character) was sufficient.

4. In the new *Codex Iuris Canonici* of 1983, the diaconate is spoken of from the standpoint of its sacramentality, introducing certain developments which deserve comment.

This is true of cann. 1008–1009. The diaconate is one of the three orders, and the CIC seems to apply to it the general theology of the sacrament of Holy Orders in its integrity.[162] If this application is valid, then it follows from it that the diaconate is a sacramental reality, of divine institution, which makes deacons *sacri ministri* (in the CIC, those who are baptized and ordained), imprints on them an "indelible character" (taking for granted what was said by Paul VI) and by reason of their consecration and deputation ("consecrantur et deputantur") renders them capable of exercising *in persona Christi Capitis* and in the grade which corresponds to them ("pro suo quisque gradu") the tasks of teaching, sanctifying and ruling, in other words the functions proper to those who are called to guide the People of God.

Integrating the diaconate within the general theology of the sacrament of Holy Orders in this way raises certain questions. Can it be theologically maintained that deacons, even *pro suo gradu*, really exercise the "munera docendi, sanctificandi et regendi" *in persona Christi Capitis* as do bishops and priests? Is that not something particular and exclusive to those who have received sacramental ordination and the consequent power to "conficere corpus et sanguinem Christi," i.e. to consecrate the Eucharist, which does not belong to deacons in any way? Should the CIC's expression *in persona Christi Capitis* be understood in a broader sense so that it can also be applied to the functions of deacons? How, then, should the Council's statement be interpreted, which says that deacons are "non ad sacerdotium, sed ad ministerium"? Can the task of "pascere populum Dei" be considered an effect of the sacramentality of the diaconate? Would not arguing over its "powers" lead to an impasse?

It is very natural that the CIC should concern itself specially and at length with the faculties proper to deacons, and it does so in several canons.[163] In can. 517, 2 and 519 deacons are mentioned with reference to cooperation with the parish priest as "pastor proprius," and to the possibility of granting them a share in the exercise of the *cura pastoralis* (can. 517, 2). This possibility of sharing in the exercise of the *cura pastoralis paroeciae* (which refers in the first place to deacons, although it can also be granted to laypeople) raises the question of the capacity of the deacon to assume the pastoral guidance of the community, and takes up again, with different nuances, what had already been established by AG 16 and *Sacrum diaconatus* V/22. Although these points referred directly to *regere*, can. 517, 2 speaks in a more nuanced way of "participatio in exercitio curae pastoralis." In any case, with reference to the possibility opened by can. 517, which is presented as a last solution, more precise thought needs to be given to the real participation of deacons, by reason of their diaconal ordination, in the "cura animarum" and the task of "pascere populum Dei."[164]

5. The recent *Catechismus Catholicae Ecclesiae* (CCE), in its definitive 1997 edition, seems to speak more decidedly in favor of the sacramentality of the diaconate.

It states that the *potestas sacra* to act *in persona Christi* only corresponds to the bishops and priests, whereas deacons hold "vim populo Dei serviendi" in their various diaconal functions (no. 875). It also mentions deacons when, concerning the sacrament of Holy Orders, it considers "ordination" as a "sacramental act" enabling recipients to exercise a "sacred power" which proceeds ultimately from Jesus Christ alone (no. 1538).

On the one hand it seems that according to the CCE deacons could also be included in a certain way in a general understanding of the sacrament of Holy Orders under some categories of the priest-hood, since it mentions them from this point of view at the same time as bishops and priests in nos. 1539–1543. On the other hand in the definitive version of no. 1554 it justifies the restriction of the term *sacerdos* to bishops and priests, excluding deacons, while maintaining that deacons also belong to the sacrament of Holy Orders (no. 1554).

Finally, the idea of sacramentality is strengthened by the explicit attribution of the doctrine of "character" to deacons as a special configuration with Christ, deacon and servant of all (no. 1570).

6. The recent *Ratio Fundamentalis* (1998), which recognizes the difficulties that exist in reaching an understanding of the "germana natura" of the diaconate, nevertheless firmly upholds the clarity of the doctrinal elements ("clarissime definita," nos. 3 and 10) on the basis of original diaconal practice and conciliar indications.

There is no doubt that we have here a way of speaking of the specific identity of the deacon which offers certain novelties in comparison with what has usually been the case up until now. The deacon has a specific configuration with Christ, Lord and Servant.[165] To this configuration there corresponds a spirituality whose distinguishing mark is "serviceability," which by ordination makes the deacon into a living "icon" of Christ the Servant in the Church (no. 11). This is offered in justification of restricting the configuration with Christ the Head and Shepherd to priests. But configuration with Christ the "Servant," and "service" as a characteristic of the ordained minister, are also valid for priests; so that it is not very clear what is "specifically diaconal" in this service, what it is that might express itself in functions or "munera" (cf. no. 9) which were the exclusive competence of deacons by reason of their sacramental capacity.

All in all, the *Ratio* clearly affirms the sacramentality of the diaconate as well as its sacramental character, in the perspective of a common theology of the sacrament of Holy Orders and the respective character which it confers.[166] Here the language is decisive and explicit, although it is not altogether clear to what extent it is the expression of more consistent theological developments or a new or better justified base.

V. Conclusion

The doctrinal position in favor of the sacramentality of the diaconate is broadly speaking the majority opinion of theologians from the twelfth century to the present day and it is taken for granted in the practice of the Church and in most documents of the Magisterium; it is upheld by those who defend the permanent diaconate (for celibate or married people) and constitutes an element that includes a large number of the propositions in favor of the diaconate for women.

Despite everything, this doctrinal position faces questions that need to be clarified more fully, either through the development of a more convincing theology of the sacramentality of the diaconate, or through a more direct and explicit intervention by the Magisterium, or by a more successful attempt to connect and harmonize the various elements. The path that was followed concerning the sacramentality of the episcopate could be taken as a decisive and instructive reference point. Among the questions requiring deeper or more fully developed theology are the following: a) the normative status of the sacramentality of the diaconate as it was fixed by the doctrinal interventions of the Magisterium, especially in Trent and in Vatican II; b) the "unity" and "oneness" of the sacrament of Holy Orders in its diverse grades; c) the exact scope of the distinction "non ad sacerdotium, sed ad ministerium (episcopi)"; d) the doctrine of the character of the diaconate and its specificity as a configuration with Christ; e) the "powers" conferred by the diaconate as a sacrament.

To reduce sacramentality to the question of *potestates* would undoubtedly be an overly narrow approach; ecclesiology offers broader and richer perspectives. But in the case of the sacrament of Holy Orders, this question cannot be passed over with the excuse that it is too narrow. The other two grades of Holy Orders, the episcopate and the priesthood, give a capacity, by reason of sacramental ordination, for tasks that an unordained person cannot perform validly. Why should it be otherwise for the diaconate? Does the difference lie in the *way* in which the *munera* are exercised or in the personal quality of the person performing them? But how could this be rendered theologically credible? If in fact these functions can be exercised by a layperson, what justification is there for the argument that they have their source in a new and distinct sacramental ordination?

The discussion of diaconal powers gives rise once again to general questions on the nature or condition of the *potestas sacra* in the Church, the connection of the sacrament of Holy Orders with the "potestas conficiendi eucharistiam," and the need to widen ecclesiological perspectives beyond a narrow view of this connection.

---

114. For these variations, see L. Ott, *Das Weihesakrament* (HbDG IV/5), Freiburg am Breisgau, 1964.

115. Peter Lombard introduced in *IV Sent.* d24 the treatise *De ordinibus ecclesiasticis* which, with the exception of certain lines, was copied from Hugh of Saint Victor (†1141), Yves of Chartres (†1040–1115) and from the *Decretum Gratiani*; all these authors depend in their turn on *De septem ordinibus ecclesiae* (5th–7th centuries), one of the first treatises of the Western Church (cf. Saint Isidore of Seville) devoted to an exposition of the competencies of the different grades of the hierarchy.

116. *IV Sent.* d24 c14.

117. Cf. *In IV Sent.* d24–25; *Suppl.* qq34–40; *SCG* IV cap. 74–77, *De art. fidei et Eccl. sacramentis.*

118. *In IV Sent.* d24 q2 a1 ad 3.

119. *Ibidem* d24 q2 a1 sol.1.

120. *Ibidem* d24 q2 a1 sol.2.

121. *Ibidem.*

122. *Ibidem* d24 q3 a2 sol.2.

123. *Ibidem* d24 q3 a2 sol.2

124. Cf. *In IV Sent.* d7 q2 ad 1; *STh* III q63 a3.

125. *In IV Sent.* d24 q1 a2 sol.2.

126. *STh* q67 a1.

127. As for the episcopate, he tended to state that it was "ordo et sacramentum, non quidem praecise distinctum a sacerdotio simplici, sed est unum sacramentum cum ipso, sicut perfectum et imperfectum." Durandus of Saint-Pourçain, *Super Sententias Comm. libri quatuor,* Parisii 1550, lib. IV d24 q6.

128. *Ibidem* q2 for what is said under a), b), c) and d).

129. *Ibidem* q3.

130. Cf. DS 1767, 1776.

131. Cf. DS 1765, 1772.

132. Cf. DS 1766, 1773.

133. Cf. DS 1765.

134. Cf. DS 1767, 1774.

135. Cf. DS 1776.

136. Cf. CT III, 682f., 686, 690; VII/II, 603, 643.

137. Cf. K. J. Becker, *Wesen und Vollmachten des Priestertums nach dem Lehramt* (QD 47), Freiburg 1970, 19–156; J. Freitag, *Sacramentum ordinis aus dem Konzil von Trient. Ausgeblendeter Dissens und erreichter Konsens,* Innsbruck 1991, 218ff.

138. Cf. *Catechismus Romanus* p. II, can. VII, q. 20.

139. Cf. F. de Vitoria, *Summa sacramentorum,* no. 226, Venice 1579, f. 136v; D. de Soto, *In Sent.* IV d. 24 q. 1 a. 4 concl. 5 (633ab).

140. Cf. R. Bellarminus, *Controversiarum de sacramento ordinis liber unicus,* in *Opera omnia* V, Paris 1873, 26.

141. *Ibidem* 27–28.

142. *Ibidem,* 30.

143. Cf., in favor: AS II/II, 227f., 314f., 317f., 359, 431, 580; raising doubts about or calling into question the sacramentality of the diaconate, AS II/II, 378, 406, 447f.

144. "Quod attinet ad Act. 6, 1–6, inter exegetas non absolute constat viros de quibus ibi agitur diaconis nostris correspondere . . ." AS III/I, 260.

145. "de indole sacramentali diaconatus, statutum est, postulantibus pluribus . . . eam in schemate caute indicare, quia in Traditione et Magisterio fundatur. Cf. praeter canonem citatum Tridentini: Pius XII, Const. Apost. *Sacramentum Ordinis,* DS 3858f. . . . Ex altera tamen parte cavetur ne Concilium paucos illos recentes auctores, qui de hac re dubia moverunt, condemnare videatur," *ibidem.*

146. Cf. AS III/I, 260–264; AS III/II, 214–218.

147. The original text said: "in ministerio episcopi." On the origin of and variations on this formula, cf. A. Kerkvoorde, *Esquisse d'une théologie du diaconat,* in: Winninger and Y. Congar (eds), *Le Diacre dans l'Eglise et le*

monde d'aujourd'hui (UnSa 59), Paris 1966, 163–171, which, for its part, includes the warning that "it would be a mistake . . . to make it [sc. this formula] the basis for a future theology of the diaconate."

148. The expression is ambiguous "nam sacerdotium est ministerium," AS III/VIII, 101.

149. The words of the *Statuta* are interpreted as follows: "significant diaconos non ad corpus et sanguinem Domini offerendum sed ad *servitium caritatis* in Ecclesia," *ibidem.*

150. "Christus . . . consecrationis missionisque suae per Apostolos suos, eorum successores, videlicet Episcopos participes effecit, qui *munus ministerii sui,* vario gradu, variis subiectis in Ecclesia legitime tradiderunt." LG 28a.

151. "Sic *ministerium ecclesiasticum* divinitus institutum diversis ordinibus exercetur ab illis qui iam ab antiquo Episcopi, Presbyteri, Diaconi vocantur," *ibidem.*

152. DS 1765. 1776.

153. Cf. the different references to Trent in the conciliar debates. Some identified *ministri* with *diaconi,* although their semantic equivalence does not justify making an instant theological identification between the two; others considered it to have been *dogmatically* defined at Trent that the diaconate constitutes the third grade of the hierarchy, but this evaluation seems to go beyond what was intended at Trent. Cf. notes 136 and 143 *supra.*

154. Cf. AS III/I, 260.

155. Cf. AAS 59 (1967) 698.

156. Cf. *ibidem* 702.

157. Cf. AAS 64 (1972) 536. 534. 537.

158. Cf. J. Beyer, *Nature et position du sacerdoce,* in: NRTh 76 (1954) 356–373, 469–480; *idem, De diaconatu animadversiones,* in: Periodica 69 (1980) 441–460.

159. Beyer especially disagreed with G. Philips' evaluation of this caution. Given that the Council wished to act *non dogmatice, sed pastorale,* even a much more explicit statement would not *ipso facto* imply condemnation of the contrary opinion. Hence in Beyer's view the reason for this caution was due to the fact that in what concerned the sacramentality of the diaconate the *haesitatio* was indeed "manifesta et doctrinalis quidem."

160. According to Beyer, the term *ministri* had a generic sense; it had not been intended to give a dogmatic statement only of what the Protestant reform refused. The sense in which Trent was now invoked often went "ultra eius in Concilio Tridentino pondus et sensum."

161. The biggest reason for this uncertainty lay in the fact of affirming "diaconum non ad sacerdotium sed ad ministerium ordinari, atque nihil in hoc ministerio agere diaconum quin et laicus idem facere non possit."

162. "Sacramento ordinis ex divina institutione inter christifideles quidam, charactere indelebili suo signantur, constituuntur sacri ministri, qui nempe consecrantur et deputantur ut, pro suo quisque gradu, in persona Christi Capitis munera docendi, sanctificandi et regendi adimplentes, Dei populum pascant." CIC can. 1008.

163. In can. 757. 764. 766. 767 (the homily is reserved "sacerdoti aut diacono," while laypeople may also be admitted "ad praedicandum"); 835. 861. 910. 911. 1003 (deacons are not ministers of the anointing of the sick, for "unctionem infirmorum valide administrat omnis et solus sacerdos": is this an application of the principle which speaks of deacons as "non ad sacerdotium, sed ad ministerium"?); 1079. 1081. 1108. 1168. 1421. 1425. 1428. 1435 (they can be "judges," something which forms part of the power of governance or jurisdiction).

164. Such reflection is necessary, because the principle is maintained that the *pastor proprius* and the final moderator of the *plena cura animarum* can only be one who has received ordination to the priesthood (the *sacerdos*). This raises the possibility of an extreme case of a *sacerdos* (who is not in fact a *parochus*, although he has all the attributes of one) and a *diaconus* (who is a *quasi-parochus*, since he has in fact the responsibility for the *cura pastoralis*, though not in its totality because he lacks the sacramental powers relating to the Eucharist and Reconciliation).

165. "specificam configurationem cum Christo, Domino et Servo omnium . . . specificam diaconi identitatem . . . is enim, prout unici ministerii ecclesiastici particeps, est in Ecclesia specificum signum sacramentale Christi Servi," *Ratio* no. 5.

166. "prout gradus ordinis sacri, diaconatus characterem imprimit et specificam gratiam sacramentalem communicat . . . signum configurativum-distinctivum animae modo indelebili impressum, quod . . . configurat Christo, qui diaconus, ideoque servus omnium, factus est," *Ratio* no. 7.

Chapter 5

The Restoration of the
Permanent Diaconate
at Vatican II

In three places, Vatican II uses different terms to describe what it
intends to do when it speaks of the diaconate as a stable rank
of the hierarchy of the Church. *Lumen Gentium* 29b uses the
notion of *restitutio*,[167] *Ad Gentes* 16f uses that of *restauratio*,[168] while
Orientalium Ecclesiarum 17 employs the word *instauratio*.[169] All
three connote the idea of restoring, renewing, re-establishing,
and re-activating. In the present chapter two points will be dealt with.
First, it is important to know the reasons why the Council restored
the permanent diaconate, and second, to examine the figure it wished
to bestow upon it.

I. THE INTENTIONS OF THE COUNCIL

The idea of re-establishing the diaconate as a permanent grade
of the hierarchy did not originate with Vatican II. It was already
current before the Second World War but was developed as a definite
possibility after 1945, especially in German-speaking countries.[170]
The challenge of responding to the pastoral needs of communities
at a time when priests were facing imprisonment, deportation,
or death led to serious consideration being given to this idea. Various
specialists soon produced studies on the theological and historical
aspects of the diaconate.[171] Some men who were thinking about
a vocation to the diaconate even established a group called the
"Community of the Diaconate."[172] A renewed theology of the Church
issuing from biblical, liturgical and ecumenical movements opened

up the way to the possibility of restoring the diaconate as a stable order of the hierarchy.[173]

Thus on the eve of the Council the idea of a permanent diaconate was very much alive in certain significant sectors of the Church and influenced a certain number of bishops and experts during the Council.

The motivations that led Vatican II to open the possibility of restoring the permanent diaconate are mainly given in the Dogmatic Constitution on the Church *Lumen Gentium* and the Decree on the missionary activity of the Church *Ad Gentes*. Because of the doctrinal nature of *Lumen Gentium*, the origin of its formulations concerning the permanent diaconate will be considered first.

During the first stage of the Council (1962)[174] the question of the diaconate did not attract much attention as a particular topic: this led certain Council Fathers to point to the absence of all mention of the diaconate in the chapter dealing with the episcopate and the priesthood.[175] But during the first intersession (1962–1963), a certain number of Council Fathers began to evoke the possibility of a restoration of the permanent diaconate, some pointing out its advantages in the missionary or ecumenical field, others recommending caution. However, most of them addressed practical questions rather than theoretical matters: they discussed in particular the question of the admission of married men and its consequences for the celibacy of the clergy.[176]

In comparison with the level of discussion of the first period, that of the second period (1963) covered more ground and proved essential for an understanding of the Council's intentions.[177] Three interventions on the permanent diaconate could be considered "foundational" in the sense that they established in some measure the directions and the parameters, both doctrinal and practical, which were taken in the course of the debate. These interventions were those of Cardinals Julius Döpfner,[178] Joannes Landazuri Ricketts,[179] and Leo Joseph Suenens.[180] The other interventions took up themes that had been raised by these three.

Beginning with the Council Fathers who favored the re-establishment of a permanent diaconate, it should be said that they stressed the fact that the Council was only examining the *possibility* of re-establishing the permanent diaconate at the time and in the places that the competent ecclesiastical authority should judge opportune. There was no indication to the effect that the establishment of a permanent diaconate might be something *obligatory* on all local Churches. The same contributors considered how the Church would benefit from such a decision from a practical and pastoral viewpoint. The presence of permanent deacons could help to resolve some of the pastoral problems caused by the shortage of priests in mission countries and in areas subject to persecution.[181] The encouragement of vocations to the diaconate could thus give greater prominence to the priesthood.[182] It could also help to improve the ecumenical relations of the Latin Church with the other Churches which have preserved the permanent diaconate.[183] Additionally, men who wanted to commit themselves more deeply to the apostolate, or those who were already engaged in a certain form of ministry could belong to the hierarchy.[184] Finally, the admission of married men to the diaconate could mean that the celibacy of priests shone out more clearly as a charism embraced in a spirit of freedom.[185]

The interventions also pointed to the theological basis for a re-establishing of the permanent diaconate. Some Council Fathers highlighted the fact that the question of the permanent diaconate was not merely a disciplinary matter, but was properly speaking a theological one.[186] As a rank within the sacred hierarchy of the Church, the diaconate had been part of the constitution of the Church from its beginnings.[187] Cardinal Döpfner stated vigorously: "Schema nostrum, agens de hierarchica constitutione Ecclesiae, ordinem diaconatus nullo modo silere potest, quia tripartitio hierarchiae ratione ordinis habita in episcopatum, presbyteratum et diaconatum est juris divini et constitutioni Ecclesiae essentialiter propria."[188] If the Council revived the permanent diaconate, it would not be altering the constitutive elements of the Church, but would only be reintroducing something that had been left aside. The teaching of the Council of Trent (Session 23, can. 17) was often invoked. Moreover, the Fathers maintained that the diaconate was a sacrament conferring grace and a character.[189] A deacon should not be considered as the same as a layman who was in the service of

the Church, because the diaconate confers the grace to exercise
a particular office.[190] Thus a deacon is not a layman who has been
raised to a higher degree of the lay apostolate, but a member of
the hierarchy by reason of sacramental grace and the character received
at the moment of ordination. But as it was assumed that permanent
deacons would live and work in the middle of the lay population
and the secular world, they could exercise the role of "bridge or
mediation between the hierarchy and the faithful."[191] Thus there was
the intention on the part of the Fathers to restore the diaconate as
a permanent rank of the hierarchy destined to penetrate secular society
in the same way as laypeople. The permanent diaconate was not
perceived as a call to the priesthood, but as a distinct ministry in the
service of the Church.[192] It could thus be a sign of the Church's
vocation to be the servant of Christ and of God.[193] The presence of
the deacon, consequently, could renew the Church in the evangelical
spirit of humility and service.

These opinions in favor of the restoration of the diaconate
met with objections. Certain Fathers underlined the fact that the
permanent diaconate would not be useful in resolving the shortage
of priests because deacons cannot replace priests completely.[194]
A number expressed the fear that the fact of accepting married men
as deacons might endanger the celibacy of priests.[195] It would create
a group of clergy inferior to the members of secular institutes, who
took a vow of chastity.[196] The Fathers suggested solutions that seemed
less prejudicial, such as giving a share of pastoral work to a larger
number of men and women, committed laypeople and members of
secular institutes.[197]

The definitive text of *Lumen Gentium,* promulgated on
21 November 1964, expresses some objectives which the Council set
in re-establishing the diaconate as a proper and permanent rank of
the hierarchy in the Latin Church.[198]

In the first place, according to no. 28a of LG, Vatican II
re-established the diaconate as a proper and permanent rank of the
hierarchy in recognition of the divinely established ecclesiastical
ministry, just as it had evolved in the course of history. Hence a motive
of faith, namely the recognition of the gift of the Holy Spirit in the
complex reality of Holy Orders, furnished the ultimate justification for
the Council's decision to re-establish the diaconate.

LG 29, however, presented what might be termed the "circumstantial reason" for the restoration of the permanent diaconate.[199] Vatican II foresaw deacons as engaging in tasks (*munera*) which were very necessary to the life of the Church (*ad vitam ecclesiae summopere necessaria*) but which in many regions could be fulfilled only with difficulty because of the discipline of the Latin Church as it existed at the time. The present difficulties caused by the shortage of priests demanded some response. Care for the faithful (*pro cura animarum*) was the determining factor in re-establishing the permanent diaconate in a local Church. The re-establishment of the permanent diaconate was therefore intended to respond to pastoral needs which were grave, not merely peripheral ones. This explains in part why it was the responsibility of the territorial episcopal conferences, and not the Pope, to determine if it was opportune to ordain such deacons, because they would have a more immediate grasp of the needs of the local Churches.

Indirectly, Vatican II was also to initiate a clarification of the identity of the priest, who did not have to fulfill all the tasks necessary to the life of the Church. In consequence, the Church would be able to experience the riches of different degrees of Holy Orders. At the same time Vatican II enabled the Church to go beyond a narrowly sacerdotal understanding of the ordained minister.[200] Since deacons were ordained "non ad sacerdotium, sed ad ministerium," it was possible to conceive of clerical life, the sacred hierarchy and ministry in the Church beyond the category of the priesthood.

It is also worth noting that the permanent diaconate could be conferred upon men of more mature age (*viris maturioris aetatis*), even upon those living in the married state, but that the law of celibacy remained intact for younger candidates. LG does not give the reasons for this decision. But the conciliar debates indicate that the Fathers wished to make of the permanent diaconate an order that would unite the sacred hierarchy and the secular life of laypeople more closely together.

Further motivations emerge from AG 16. Here it can be seen that the Council was not re-establishing the permanent diaconate merely because of a shortage of priests. There were already men who were in fact exercising the diaconal ministry. By the imposition of hands, these were "to be strengthened and more closely associated with the altar" (*corroborari et altari arctius conjungi*). The sacramental grace of the diaconate would render them capable of exercising their ministry more effectively. Here Vatican II was not motivated only by current pastoral difficulties, but by the need to recognize the existence of the diaconal ministry in certain communities. It desired to confirm by sacramental grace those who were already exercising the diaconal ministry or showing forth its charism.

From *Lumen Gentium* to *Ad Gentes,* there was a shift in the Council's intentions. These intentions can be of great importance in understanding not only the diaconate but the true nature of the sacrament. Three main reasons can be discerned in favor of the restoration of the permanent diaconate. In the first place, the restoration of the diaconate as a proper degree of Holy Orders enabled the constitutive elements of the sacred hierarchy willed by God to be recognized. Secondly, it was a response to the need to guarantee indispensable pastoral care to communities which had been deprived of this because of a shortage of priests. Finally, it was a confirmation, a reinforcement and a more complete incorporation into the ministry of the Church of those who were already *de facto* exercising the ministry of deacons.

II. The Form of the Permanent Diaconate Restored by Vatican II

Six of the documents promulgated by Vatican II contain some teachings concerning the diaconate: *Lumen Gentium, Ad Gentes, Dei Verbum, Sacrosanctum Concilium, Orientalium Ecclesiarum* and *Christus Dominus.* The following paragraphs will cover the key elements of the teaching of Vatican II in order to identify more precisely the form or "figure" of the permanent diaconate which has been restored.

1. Vatican II recognized the diaconate as one of the sacred Orders. LG 29a established that deacons belong to the lowest degree of the hierarchy (*in gradu inferiori hierarchiae sistunt diaconi*). They are "sustained by sacramental grace" (*gratia sacramentali roborati*) and receive the imposition of hands "non ad sacerdotium, sed ad

ministerium." But this important expression, drawn from the *Statuta Ecclesiae antiqua,* and a variation on a still more ancient expression from the *Traditio Apostolica* of Hippolytus, is not explained anywhere in the conciliar documents.[201]

Vatican II taught that Christ instituted the sacred ministries for the nurturing and constant growth of the People of God. Those ministers are endowed with a sacred power to serve the Body of Christ, so that all may arrive at salvation (LG 18a). Like the other sacred ministers, deacons should therefore consecrate themselves to the growth of the Church and the pursuit of its plan of salvation.

Within the body of ministers, bishops, who possess the fullness of the priesthood, have taken up the service of the community, presiding in place of God over the flock as teachers, priests and shepherds. Deacons, with the priests, help the bishops in their ministry (LG 20c). Belonging to the lowest order of the ministry, deacons grow in holiness through the faithful fulfillment of their ministry as a share in the mission of Christ, the Supreme Priest. "Missionis autem et gratiae supreme Sacerdotis peculiari modo participes sunt inferioris quoque ordinis ministri, imprimis Diaconi, qui mysteriis Christi et ecclesiae servientes . . ." (LG 41d) Although they occupy different ranks within the hierarchy, all three orders deserve to be called ministers of salvation (AG 16a), exercising one single ecclesiastical ministry in the hierarchical communion. Strictly speaking deacons belong to the mission of Christ but not to that of the bishop or to that of the priest. However, the specific ways of exercising this participation are determined by the demands of the communion within the hierarchy. Far from degrading the orders of priest and deacon within the hierarchy, hierarchical communion situates them within the single mission of Christ, shared in by the different orders in different degrees.

2. The functions assigned to deacons by the Council also provide indications concerning the way it envisaged the diaconal order. It is good to remember that the basic function of all the sacred ministers, according to Vatican II, is to nurture the People of God and lead them to salvation. Thus LG 29b declared that the permanent diaconate can be re-established if the competent authorities decide that it is opportune to choose deacons, even from among married men,

pro cura animarum. All the tasks that deacons are authorized to fulfill are at the service of the basic duty of building up the Church and taking care of the faithful.

As for their specific tasks, LG 29a presented the service which the deacon renders to the People of God in terms of the triple ministry of the liturgy, the word, and charity. The particular tasks of the deacon are seen as falling within the framework of one or another of these ministries. The ministry of the liturgy, or sanctification, is developed at length in *Lumen Gentium.* It includes the faculty of administering Baptism solemnly (cf. SC 68), of being custodian and dispenser of the Eucharist, assisting at and blessing weddings in the name of the Church, bringing Viaticum to the dying, presiding over the worship and prayer of the faithful, administering sacramentals, and finally officiating at funeral and burial services. The function of teaching includes reading the Sacred Scripture to the faithful, and instructing and exhorting the people. DV 25a and SC 35 include deacons among those who are officially engaged in the ministry of the word. The ministry of "government" is not mentioned as such, but rather termed the ministry of charity. Administration is at least mentioned.

It is clear that the function of the deacon as described by *Lumen Gentium* is above all liturgical and sacramental. Questions inevitably arise about the specific notion of diaconal ordination "non ad sacerdotium sed ad ministerium." The form of the diaconal ministry based on *Lumen Gentium* invites a deeper exploration of the meaning of *sacerdotium* and *ministerium.*

Ad Gentes gave a different configuration to the permanent diaconate, as can be seen by looking at the functions it assigned to it, probably because it sprang from the experience of mission territories. In the first place, *Ad Gentes* contained little about the liturgical ministry of the deacon. Preaching the word of God was mentioned in connection with catechism teaching. What is called the ministry of "government" received broader treatment in AG 16f. Deacons preside over scattered Christian communities in the name of the parish priest and the bishop. They also practice charity in social or relief work.

Vatican II showed some hesitation in its description of the permanent diaconate which it was restoring. In the more doctrinal perspective of *Lumen Gentium,* it tended to place the emphasis on the liturgical image of the deacon and his ministry of sanctification. In the missionary perspective of *Ad Gentes,* the focus shifted toward the administrative, charitable aspect of the figure of the deacon and his ministry of government. It is however interesting to note that nowhere did the Council claim that the form of the permanent diaconate which it was proposing was a restoration of a previous form. This explains why certain theologians avoid the term "restoration," because it might easily suggest something being brought back to its original state. But Vatican II never aimed to do that. What it re-established was *the principle of the permanent exercise of the diaconate,* and not one particular form which the diaconate had taken in the past.[202] Having established the possibility of re-establishing the permanent diaconate, the Council seemed open to the kind of form it might take in the future, in function of pastoral needs and ecclesial practice, but always in fidelity to Tradition. Vatican II could not be expected to provide a clearly defined picture of the permanent diaconate, because of the gap that existed in the pastoral life of those times, unlike the case of the episcopate or the priesthood. The most it could do was to open the possibility of reinstalling the diaconate as a proper, permanent degree in the hierarchy and as a stable way of life, give some general theological principles even though they might appear timid, and establish some general norms of practice. Beyond that it could do no more than wait for the contemporary form of the permanent diaconate to develop. Finally, the apparent indecision and hesitancy of the Council might serve as an invitation to the Church to continue working to discern the type of ministry appropriate to the diaconate through ecclesial practice, canonical legislation, and theological reflection.[203]

---

167. "diaconatus in futurum tamquam proprius ac permanens gradus hierarchiae restitui poterit," LG 29b.

168. "ordo diaconatus ut status vitae permanens restauretur ad normam constitutionis de ecclesia," AG 16f.

169. "exoptat haec sancta synodus, ut institutum diaconatus permanentis, ubi in desuetudinem venerit, instauretur," OE 17.

170. Cf. J. Hornef and Winninger, *Chronique de la restauration du diaconat (1945–1965)*, in: Winninger and Y. Congar (eds), *Le Diacre dans l'Eglise*, 205–222.

171. A huge dossier of theological and historical studies, edited by K. Rahner and H. Vorgrimler was published in Germany, entitled *Diaconia in Christo. Uber die Erneuerung des Diakonates* (QD 15/16), Freigburg am Breisgau, 1962.

172. Cf. J. Hornef and Winninger, *Chronique*, 207–208.

173. For example, Yves Congar explored the impact of the theology of the People of God and the ontology of grace on a renewed understanding of the ministries which could open the possibility of restoring the diaconate. Cf. *Le Diaconat dans la théologie des ministères* in Winninger and Y. Congar (eds), *Le Diacre dans l'Eglise,* especially pp. 126f.

174. The Council discussed the first draft of *De Ecclesia* from the 31st General Congregation, 1 December 1962 to the 36th General Congregation, 7 December 1962.

175. Joseph Cardinal Bueno y Monreal (31 GC, 1 December 1962), *Acta Synodalia Sacrosancti Concilii Oecumenici Vaticani II* (AS), vol. 1, Pars IV, 131. Mgr. Raphael Rabban, for his part, asked why the schema made mention "de duobus gradibus ordinis, de episcopatu scilicet et de sacerdotio" and not of the diaconate "qui ad ordinem pertinet," *ibidem* 236.

176. Cf. G. Caprile, *Il Concilio Vaticano II. Il primo periodo 1962–1963*, Rome 1968, 337, 410, 413, 494, 498, 501, 536.

177. The Council discussed the chapter on the hierarchical structure of the Church from 4th to 30th October 1963.

178. Julius Cardinal Döpfner (43 GC, 7 October 1963), AS II/II, 227–230.

179. Joannes Cardinal Landazuri Ricketts (43 GC, 8 October 1963), *ibidem* 314–317.

180. Leo Joseph Cardinal Suenens (43 GC, 8 October 1963), *ibidem* 317–320.

181. Cf. Mgr Franciscus Seper (44 GC, 9 October 1963), *ibidem* 359; Mgr. Bernardus Yago (45 GC, 10 October 1963), *ibidem* 406; Mgr. Joseph Clemens Maurer (45 GC, written intervention), *ibidem* 412; and Mgr. Paul Yü Pin (45 GC), *ibidem* 431.

182. Cf. Paul Cardinal Richaud (44 GC, 9 October 1963), *ibidem* 346–347; Mgr. Bernardus Yago, *ibidem* 406.

183. Mgr. F. Seper, *ibidem* 359.

184. Card. Landazuri Ricketts, *ibidem* 315; Card. J. Döpfner, *ibidem* 229.

185. Cf. Mgr. J. Maurer, *ibidem* 411 ; Mgr. Emmanuel Talam·s Camandari (46 GC, 11 October 1963), *ibidem* 450; and Mgr. George Kémére (47 GC, 14 October 1963), *ibidem* 534.

186. Cf. Card. J. Döpfner, *ibidem* 227; Card. J. Landazuri Ricketts, *ibidem* 314.

187. Cf. Card. L. Suenens, *ibidem* 317; Mgr. Joseph Slipyj (46 GC, 10 October 1963), *ibidem* 445.

188. Card. J. Döpfner, *ibidem* 227.

189. Cf. Mgr. Armandus Fares (47 GC, 14 October 1963), *ibidem* 530–531; Mgr. Narcissus Jubany Arnau (48 GC, 15 October 1963), *ibidem* 580; Mgr. J. Maurer, *ibidem* 411.

190. Card. J. Landazuri Ricketts, *ibidem* 314–5; Card. L. Suenens, *ibidem* 318; Mgr. Seper, *ibidem* 319.

191. Mgr. Yü Pin, *ibidem* 431.

192. Mgr. B. Yago, *ibidem* 407.

193. Mgr. J. Maurer, *ibidem* 410.

194. Anicetus Fernandez, O. (45 GC, 10 October 1963), *ibidem* 424; Mgr. Joseph Drzazga (49 GC, 16 October 1963), *ibidem* 624.

195. Mgr. Franciscus Franic (44 GC, 10 October 1963), *ibidem* 378; Mgr. Dinus Romoli (48 GC, 15 October 1963), *ibidem* 598; Mgr. Petrus Cule (47 GC, 14 October 1963), *ibidem* 518.

196. Mgr. Joseph Carraro, *ibidem* 525–526.

197. Card. F. Spellman, *ibidem* 83; A. Fernandez, *ibidem* 424; Mgr. Victorius Costantini, *ibidem* 447.

198. On 15 September 1964, Mgr. Aloysius Eduardo Henriquez Jimenez read the *relatio* explaining the text of the Doctrinal Commission on the priesthood and the diaconate, before the Fathers proceeded to vote on the chapter of LG dealing with the hierarchy. Explaining the position of the text, he stated that in the Church bishops, priests, and deacons shared in power in different ways and to different degrees. As at Trent, the text taught that the diaconate belongs to the sacred hierarchy, of which it is the lowest degree. Ordained for ministry and not for the priesthood, deacons have received sacramental grace and have been charged with a triple service of the liturgy, of the word, and of charity. The diaconate could be conferred on married men. Cf. AS III/II, 211–218. Mgr. Franciscus Franic presented the opposing views, *ibidem* 193–201.

199. K. Rahner, *L'Enseignement de Vatican II sur le diaconat et sa restauration,* in Winninger and Y. Congar (eds), *Le Diacre dans l'Eglise,* 227.

200. Cf. A. Borras and B. Pottier, *La Grâce du diaconat,* Brussels 1998, 22–40.

201. Cf. A. Kerkvoorde, *Esquisse d'une théologie du diaconat,* in Winninger and Y. Congar (eds), *Le Diacre dans l'Eglise,* 157–171.

202. A. Borras and B. Pottier, *op. cit.,* 20.

203. Cf. A. Kerkvoorde, *op. cit.,* 155–156.

Chapter 6

The Reality of the Permanent Diaconate Today

More than 40 years after Vatican II, what is the reality of the permanent diaconate?

To examine the available statistics is to realize the huge disparity that exists in the distribution of deacons around the world. Out of a total of 25,122 deacons in 1998,[204] North America alone accounts for 12,801, i.e. just over half (50.9%), while Europe has 7,864 (31.3%): this means a total of 20,665 deacons (82.2%) in the industrialized countries of the northern hemisphere. The remaining 17.8% are distributed as follows: South America 2,370 (9.4%); Central America and the Caribbean 1,387 (5.5%); Africa 307 (1.22%); Asia 219 (0.87%). Finally comes Australasia and the Pacific, with 174 deacons or 0.69% of the total.[205]

One very striking point is that it is in the advanced industrialized countries of the North[206] that the diaconate has developed particularly. Now that was not at all what the Council Fathers envisaged when they asked for a "reactivation" of the permanent diaconate. They expected, rather, that there would be a rapid increase among the young Churches of Africa and Asia, where pastoral work relied on a large number of lay catechists.[207] But they had laid down that it would pertain "to the competent territorial bodies of bishops, of one kind or another, with the approval of the Supreme Pontiff, to decide whether and where it [was] opportune for such deacons to be established for the care of souls" (LG 29b). It is therefore not surprising that the diaconate did not develop uniformly throughout the Church, since the evaluation of the needs of the People of God made by the different episcopates could vary according to the specific circumstances of the Churches and their modes of organization.

What these statistics enable us to see is that there were two very different situations to be dealt with. On the one hand, after the Council most of the Churches in Western Europe and North America were faced with a steep reduction in the numbers of priests and had to undertake a major reorganization of ministries. On the other hand, the Churches that were mainly in former mission territories had long since adopted a structure which relied on the commitment of large numbers of laypeople, the catechists.

These two typical situations need to be studied separately, without losing sight of the fact that many variations exist; and also that in both cases, a certain number of bishops may have wanted to institute the permanent diaconate in their dioceses not so much for pastoral reasons as from a theological motive which had also been invoked by Vatican II: to enable the ordained ministry to be expressed better, through the three degrees traditionally recognized.

FIRST TYPICAL SITUATION: CHURCHES WITH A LOW NUMBER OF DEACONS

Many Churches, then, did not feel the need to develop the permanent diaconate. These were mainly Churches that had long since been accustomed to function with a restricted number of priests and to rely on the commitment of a very large number of laypeople, mainly as catechists. The case of Africa is an example in this regard.[208] It is undoubtedly matched by the experience of other young Churches.

It will be remembered that in the 1950s many missionaries and bishops in Africa had asked for the reactivation of the diaconate while thinking particularly of the catechists in mission countries. They saw it as a way of responding to the liturgical demands of the missions and the shortage of priests. These new deacons would thus be able to take care of the liturgy in the branch churches, lead the Sunday gatherings in the absence of the missionary, officiate at funerals, assist at weddings, look after catechesis and the proclamation of the Word of God, take charge of *caritas* and the Church administration, confer certain sacraments, and so on.[209] This perspective was what many Council Fathers had in mind at Vatican II when, in *Ad Gentes*, the Council referred to "the ranks of men and women catechists, well-deserving of missionary work to the nations."[210]

But in the years that followed the Council, the African bishops displayed considerable reservations and did not undertake the road to the reactivation of the diaconate. A participant at the eighth Kinshasa theological week held in 1973 noted that the proposal for a restoration of the permanent diaconate in Africa raised much more opposition than enthusiasm. The objections raised would be widely repeated elsewhere. They had to do with deacons' state in life, the financial situation of the young churches, the consequences on vocations to the actual priesthood, confusion and uncertainty about the nature of the diaconal vocation, the clericization of laypeople who were committed to the apostolate, the conservatism and lack of critical spirit of certain candidates, the marriage of clergy and the depreciation of celibacy, and the reaction of faithful who would content themselves with the diaconate as a sort of half-measure.[211]

The Congolese bishops therefore adopted an attitude of caution. Why should catechists be ordained as deacons if no new power was being given to them? They decided that it would be preferable to embark on a revaluation of the lay state, and work to renew the role of catechists. Other countries would appeal for a greater participation of laypeople as "servants of the Word" or activity leaders of small communities. That could be done all the better now that the Council had so strongly highlighted the vocation of all the baptized to share in the Church's mission.

An often heard objection, therefore, was "What can a deacon do that a layman can't?" It has to be recognized that the sacramental link that joins deacons to their bishop creates special, lifelong obligations for the bishop which can be difficult to manage, especially in the case of married deacons.[212] Furthermore, it is normally a question of Churches in which the place of the ordained ministry is well defined and retains its full meaning, even though priests may be few in number.

That said, it is nevertheless worth mentioning initiatives such as that of the bishop of the Native American diocese of San Cristobal (Mexico), Monsignor Ruiz. Faced with the fact that his diocese had never succeeded in producing vocations to the priesthood among the indigenous Indians, he decided to undertake an intensive promotion of the permanent diaconate. Accordingly he put in place a long process of formation designed to lead married Native American men to the diaconate. These would thus be sacramentally associated to his episcopal ministry and form the beginnings of an indigenous Church.[213]

SECOND TYPICAL SITUATION: CHURCHES WHERE THE DIACONATE IS MORE DEVELOPED

The second typical situation is that of the Churches where the diaconate has undergone its greatest expansion. These are the Churches which have had to face a considerable drop in the number of priests: the United States, Canada, Germany, Italy, France, etc. The need to set about a reorganization of pastoral duties to respond to the needs of Christian communities which were accustomed to a wide range of services, and the obligation of finding new collaborators, all helped to stimulate the emergence of new ministries and an increase in the number of laypeople working full time on parish or diocesan pastoral work.[214] This also favored the expansion of the diaconate. But at the same time it exercised a very strong pressure on the kind of tasks that were entrusted to deacons. Tasks which for a long time had been undertaken by priests without any problem because of their large numbers, now had to be given to other collaborators, some ordained (the deacons), others not ordained (lay pastoral officials). Because of this background the diaconate often came to be seen as a *supply ministry for the priesthood.*

This dynamic is reflected in the results of a broad study undertaken in the United States,[215] which is clearly representative of the situation existing in many countries. The study shows that deacons are mainly doing what priests used to do unaided before the restoration of the diaconate. They exercise their ministry in the parish where they live, and there they fulfill mainly liturgical and sacramental functions. Their parish priests find them particularly useful in sacramental activities such as baptisms, weddings, and liturgical acts. The same applies to the care of the sick and homilies. The field in which they take least part is in the ministry to prisoners and the promotion of civil rights and human rights. Lay leaders, for their part, consider that deacons are most successful in more familiar and traditional roles such as the liturgy and the administration of the sacraments. And it is predicted that the number of deacons will increase because of the reduction in the numbers of priests. Thus, as they accomplish tasks traditionally fulfilled by priests, there may be a danger of deacons being seen as "incomplete priests" or else as "more advanced laymen." The danger is the greater since the first generations of deacons have received much less detailed theological training than that of priests or that of pastoral officials.

A similar development is also to be found in other areas that likewise suffer from a marked reduction in the numbers of priests.[216] It is the result of an effort to respond to the real needs of the People of God. It enables these Churches to guarantee a wider presence of the ordained ministry within Christian communities which are in danger of losing sight of the real meaning of that ministry. Together with the bishop and the priest, the deacon will remind them that it is Christ who is the foundation of the Church in every place and that through the Spirit he is still acting in the Church today.

In this context, however, the identity of the deacon tends to take the figure of the priest as a reference point; the deacon is perceived as the person who helps or replaces the priest in activities that previously he carried out in person. Many consider this development to be problematical, because it makes it more difficult for the diaconal ministry to evolve an identity of its own.[217] For this reason, here and there, efforts are made to modify this development by identifying charisms which might be those proper to the diaconate and tasks which might suitably belong primarily to the diaconate.

LINES OF DEVELOPMENT

For their part, the most recent texts from the Roman Congregations list the tasks which can be entrusted to deacons, and group them under the three recognized diakonias, namely those of the liturgy, the word, and charity.[218] Even when it is considered that one or other of these diakonias could take up the greater part of a deacon's activity, it is insisted on that the three diakonias taken together "represent a unity in the service of the divine plan of Redemption: the ministry of the word leads to ministry at the altar, which in turn prompts the transformation of life by the liturgy, resulting in charity."[219] But it is recognized that in these tasks taken all together, "the service of charity"[220] is to be seen as particularly characteristic of the deacons' ministry.

In many regions, then, efforts have been made to identify
a certain number of tasks for deacons which can be connected in one
way or another to the "service of charity." Particular advantage may
be taken of the fact that most of them are married men, earning their
own living, immersed in the world of work, and, together with their
wives, contributing their own life experience.[221]

For example, a text by the bishops of France published in
1970 expressed their preference "for deacons who, in daily contact with
others through their family and work situation, can witness with their
whole lives to the service that the People of God should render to
men, following Christ's example. . . . Permanent deacons will thus
share in their own special way in the efforts of the hierarchical Church
to go out to meet unbelief and poverty, and to be more fully present
in the world. They will keep all previous commitments which are
compatible with the diaconal ministry."[222] The mission entrusted to
them, therefore, may often be situated "in the sphere of work and
association or trade-union life (or even political life, particularly at the
level of local government). Their mission is directed toward the care of
the poor and marginalized in such places, but also in their own district
and their parish, starting with home and family life."[223]

Hence in various places particular efforts have been made
to make the diaconate a "threshold ministry," which aims to look after
"the frontier Church": work in surroundings where the priest is not
present, and also with one-parent families, couples, prisoners, young
people, drug addicts, Aids victims, the elderly, disadvantaged groups,
etc. The tasks of deacons may be oriented toward activities in the
social, charitable or administrative spheres, without, however, neglecting
the necessary link with liturgical and teaching duties. In Latin
America, the focus is placed upon families who proclaim the Gospel
in the midst of zones of conflict; a presence in extreme situations such
as drugs, prostitution and urban violence; an active presence in the
sector of education, the world of work and the professional sphere;
a greater presence in densely populated zones and likewise in the
countryside; and finally, leadership given in small communities.[224] Very
often, efforts are directed toward ensuring that these deacons receive
progressively more thorough theological and spiritual formation.

The outcome of all this very diverse experience makes it
clear that it is not possible to characterize the totality of the diaconal

ministry by delineating tasks that belong exclusively to deacons because of ecclesial tradition—which is far from clear—or through a rigid distribution of tasks among the different ministers.[225] A text of Vatican II seems to have intuited this, since one of the reasons it invoked for re-establishing "the diaconate as a permanent state of life" was to strengthen, "by the imposition of hands transmitted from the apostles" and to unite more closely to the altar, "men who *accomplish a truly diaconal ministry,* either by preaching the word of God, or by governing far-off Christian communities in the name of the parish priest and bishop, or by exercising charity in social or charitable works" (AG 16 f).[226] All of this leads certain people to propose that in order to define the character of the diaconate it is necessary to look rather at the *being* of the deacon. "It is in the aspect of *being* that the specificity of the permanent diaconate is to be sought, and not in the aspect of *doing*. It is what they *are* that gives its true meaning to what they do."[227]

It is in this perspective of configuration to Christ the Servant that theological and pastoral studies on the lines of development of the permanent diaconate are currently being made. This theological given is seen as providing the opportunity for an in-depth spiritual reflection that is particularly appropriate for the present era. It can also provide guidance to pastors in their choice of the tasks to entrust to deacons. In that case, the tasks selected for them will preferably be such as to highlight this particular characteristic of the diaconate. These will naturally include service to the poor and oppressed; a service that is not limited to mere assistance but which, following Christ's own example, will be a sharing of life with the poor in order to journey with them toward their total liberation.[228] Their tasks will include service to those who are on the threshold of the Church and who need to be led to the Eucharist. In many countries this perspective is prominent in the minds of those responsible for deacons' formation, and a spirituality and a pastoral practice of the "service of charity" can be seen to develop in the deacons themselves. The true figure of the deacon should thus emerge little by little in the performance of various ministries, and be manifest through a definite way of doing—in the spirit of service—what all are called to do, but also through a pronounced dedication to particular tasks or functions which make Christ the Servant ever more visible.

However, it seems to be an established fact that the development of the diaconal ministry must always be thought of in relation to the real needs of the Christian community. Certain Churches will not feel the need to develop it very widely. Other Churches will, on occasions, require the deacons to perform tasks other than those listed above; here one could think of those tasks that contribute to pastoral leadership in parishes and small Christian communities. The essential objective for pastors, inspired by Saint Paul, must always be that of seeing that the faithful are equipped "for the work of ministry, for building up the body of Christ, until all of us come to the unity of the faith and of the knowledge of the Son of God, to maturity, to the measure of the full stature of Christ" (Ephesians 4:12–13). At the service of the bishop and his presbyterium, the deacon should, in the way which is proper to him, go wherever pastoral care requires him to be.

---

204. These figures and the analysis of them were kindly supplied to us in the course of the Fall 1999 session of the Commission by Prof. Enrico Nenna, Ufficio centrale statistica della Chiesa, Segretaria di Stato.

205. If a comparison is made between the numbers of priests and deacons in the different continents, the same differences are observable as before. While in America as a whole there are 7.4 priests per deacon (mainly because of the high number of deacons in North America), in Asia there are 336 priests to one deacon. In Africa there are 87 priests per permanent deacon, in Europe 27, and in Australasia and the Pacific, 31. The relative weight of the deacons within the ordained ministry therefore varies greatly from one place to another.

206. Another source of information gives a list of countries where there are the greatest numbers of permanent deacons: United States (11,589), Germany (1,918), Italy (1,845), France (1,222), Canada (824), Brazil (826).

207. Cf. H. Legrand, *Le Diaconat dans sa relation à la théologie de l'Eglise et aux ministères. Réception et devenir du diaconate depuis Vatican II* in: A. Haquin and Weber (eds), *Diaconate, 21e siècle*, Brussels-Paris-Montreal, 1997, 13 and 14.

208. For the following points, cf. J. Kabasu Bamba, *Diacres permanents ou catéchistes au Congo-Kinshasa*, Ottawa 1999, duplicated text, 304 pages.

209. The author is here quoting Mgr. W. Van Bekkum, Mgr. Eugène D'Souza (India), Mgr. J. F. Cornelis (Elizabethville) and, at the time of the

preparation of the Council, the (mostly European) Ordinaries of Congo and Rwanda. *op. cit.*, 190.

210. *Decree on the missionary activity of the Church*, no. 17a. This calls to mind the interventions of Mgr. B. Yago and Mgr. Paul Yü Pin referred to in the previous chapter.

211. Cf. *op. cit.* 195, which has a reference to M. Singleton, *Les Nouvelles Formes de ministère en Afrique*, in: Pro Mundi Vita 50 (1974), 33.

212. The archbishop of Santiago de Chile reported the objections of certain priests as follows: "They say for example that the diaconate is an unnecessary commitment, since its functions can be fulfilled by laymen and laywomen for given periods of time; if it works, their mandate is prolonged, and if not, it is not renewed." Mgr C. Oviedo Cavada, *La promoción del diaconado permanente*, in: Iglesia de Santiago (Chile), no. 24 (September 1992), 25.

213. See a long text published by the diocese of San Cristobal De Las Casas, *Directorio Diocesano para el Diaconado Indìgena Permanente*, 1999, 172 pages.

214. Depending on the country, these collaborators received different names: "pastoral officials," "pastoral workers or leaders," "pastoral auxiliaries," "pastoral lay agents," "parish auxiliaries," "parish assistants," "pastoral assistants," (Pastoralassistenten und Pastoralassistentinnen), etc. Cf. A. Borras, *Des laïcs en responsabilité pastorale?* Paris 1998.

215. NCCB, *National Study of the Diaconate, Summary Report*, in: Origins, vol. 25, no. 30 (18 January 1996).

216. See for example Maskens, *Un enquête sur les diacres francophones de Belgique*, in: A. Haquin and Weber (eds), *Diaconat, 21e siècle*, 217–232.

217. Thus, B. Sesboue, *Quelle est l'identité ministérielle du diacre?* in *L'Eglise à venir*, Paris 1999, 255–257.

218. See for example the text of the Congregation for the Clergy, *Directorium pro ministerio et vita diaconorum permanentium*, February 22, 1998, published as *Directory for the Ministry and Life of Permanent Deacons*, in *The Permanent Diaconate*, London, 1998, 88.

219. *Ibidem* 39, 103. The text adds in the next paragraph: "It is important that deacons fully exercise their ministry, in preaching, in the liturgy and in charity, to the extent that circumstances permit. They should not be relegated to marginal duties, be made merely to act as substitutes, nor discharge duties normally entrusted to nonordained members of the faithful."

220. See Congregation for Catholic Education, *Basic Norms for the Formation of Permanent Deacons*, 9: "Finally the *munus regendi* is exercised in devotion to works of charity and assistance and in motivating communities or sectors of the ecclesial life, especially in what has to do with charity. *This is the*

ministry which is most characteristic of the deacon" (emphasis added). In *The Permanent Diaconate*, 1998, p.27.

221. "It is not the wife who is ordained and nevertheless the mission entrusted to the deacon obliges the couple to redefine themselves in some way, in function of this ministry," M. Cacouet and B. Viole, *Les diacres*, quoted in a study document on the role of the deacon's wife, Quebec 1993. For this reason, in many countries the wife joins her husband for the initial training period and takes part in continued training activities with him.

222. Note of the Episcopal Commission for the Clergy, cited by F. Deniau, *Mille diacres en France*, in: *Etudes* 383, 5 (1995), 526.

223. *Art cit.*, 527. This direction taken by the bishops was confirmed in 1996 during their gathering at Lourdes, where they expressed their desire that "the image given by deacons should not be that of supplying for priests, but of communion with them in the exercise of the sacrament of Holy Orders." *"Points d'attention . . .,"* in: *Documentation Catholique* no. 2149 (1996), 1012–1013.

224. J. G. Mesa Angulo, OP, *Aportes para visualizar un horizonte pastoral para el diaconado permanente en América Latina, hacia el tercer milenio*, in: Celam, *I Congreso de diaconado permanente*, Lima, August 1998. Working document.

225. A certain number of tasks, of course, are reserved to deacons by Canon Law, but they do not account for the whole of the deacon's activity.

226. Emphasis added.

227. R. Page, *Diaconat permanent et diversité des ministères. Perspectives du Droit Canonique*, Montreal 1988, 61.

228. V. Gerardi, *El diaconado en la Iglesia*, in: Celam, *op. cit.*, p. 8, referring to the First International Congress held in Turin in 1977.

Chapter 7

Theological Approach to the Diaconate in the Wake of Vatican II

A theological approach to the diaconate in the wake of Vatican II should start from the Council texts, examine how they were received and how they were later enlarged upon in the documents of the Magisterium, take account of the fact that the restoration of the diaconate was accomplished very unevenly in the post-Conciliar period, and above all pay special attention to the doctrinal fluctuations that have closely shadowed the various pastoral suggestions. Today there are numerous very different aspects which require an effort at doctrinal clarification. This chapter will attempt to contribute to these efforts at clarification as follows. First it will pinpoint the roots and reasons that make the theological and ecclesial identity of the diaconate (both permanent and transitory) into a real "quaestio disputata" in certain respects. Then it will outline a theology of the diaconal ministry, which may serve as a firm common basis to inspire the fruitful re-creation of the diaconate in Christian communities.

I. The Texts of Vatican II and the Post-Conciliar Magisterium

In the Council texts which mention the diaconate specifically (cf. SC 35, LG 20, LG 28, LG 29, LG 41, OE 17, CD 15, DV 25, AG 15, AG 16), Vatican II did not aim to offer a dogmatic decision on any of the questions debated in the course of the Council, nor to lay down a strict doctrinal system. Its true interest was in opening a path to the restoration of the permanent diaconate that could be put into effect in a plurality of ways. This is perhaps why, in the texts taken as a whole, certain fluctuations can be seen in the theology, depending on the place or context in which the diaconate is mentioned. Both with reference to pastoral priorities and in what concerns objective doctrinal difficulties, the Council texts show a diversity of theological nuances which it is quite hard to harmonize.

After the Council the theme of the diaconate was developed or referred to in other documents of the post-Conciliar Magisterium: Paul VI's Motu Proprio *Sacrum diaconatus ordinem* (1967); the Apostolic Constitution *Pontificalis romani recognitio* (1968); Paul VI's Motu Proprio *Ad Pascendum* (1972); the new *Codex Iuris Canonici* (1983); and the *Catechismus Catholicae Ecclesiae* (1992, 1997).[229] These new documents develop the basic elements of Vatican II and sometimes add important theological, ecclesial, or pastoral clarifications; but they do not all speak from the same perspective, nor at the same doctrinal level.[230] For this reason, in order to attempt a theological approach in the wake of Vatican II, it is appropriate to bear in mind the possible relation between the doctrinal fluctuations (in Vatican II texts) and the diversity of theological approaches perceptible in post-Conciliar proposals about the diaconate.

II. Implications of the Sacramentality of the Diaconate

As stated above (cf. Chapter IV), the most reliable doctrine and that most in accord with ecclesial practice is that which holds that the diaconate is a sacrament. If its sacramentality were denied, the diaconate would simply represent a form of ministry rooted in Baptism; it would take on a purely functional character, and the Church would possess a wide faculty of decision making with regard to restoring or suppressing it, and to its specific configuration. Whatever the context, the Church would have a much greater freedom of action than is granted to her over the sacraments instituted by Christ.[231] A denial of the sacramentality of the diaconate would dissipate the main reasons why the diaconate is a theologically disputed question. But to make such a denial would be to diverge from the path marked out by Vatican II. Hence it is with the sacramentality of the diaconate as a starting point that the other questions concerning the theology of the diaconate should be dealt with.

1. The diaconate as rooted in Christ

As a sacrament, the diaconate must ultimately be rooted in Christ. The Church, herself rooted in the free gift of the Blessed Trinity, has no capacity to create sacraments or to confer on them their salvific effectiveness.[232] In order to affirm that the diaconate is a sacrament, it is theologically necessary to state that it is rooted in Christ. Moreover, this fact enables us to understand the various theological attempts to link the diaconate directly to Christ himself (whether in regard to the mission of the apostles,[233] or to the washing of the feet at the Last Supper[234]). But that does not imply that it is necessary to maintain that Christ himself "instituted" the diaconate directly as a degree of the sacrament. The Church played a decisive role in its specific historical establishment. That fact was implicitly recognized in the opinion (a minority one today) that identified the institution of the Seven (cf. Acts of the Apostles 6:1–6) with the first deacons.[235] This has emerged clearly from the exegetical and theological studies on the complex of historical developments and the progressive differentiation of ministries and charisms, finally arriving at the tripartite structure of bishop, priest, and deacon.[236] The cautious language used by Trent ("divina ordinatione") and Vatican II ("divinitus institutum . . . iam ab antiquo . . .")[237] reflects the impossibility of totally identifying Christ's and the Church's activity with relation to the sacraments, and also reflects the complexity of the historical facts.

2. The sacramental "character" of the diaconate and its "configuration" with Christ

Vatican II makes no explicit statement about the sacramental character of the diaconate; however, the post-Conciliar documents do. These speak of the "indelible character" linked to the stable condition of service (*Sacrum Diaconatus*, 1967) or of an imprint that cannot be removed and which configures the deacon to Christ, who made himself the "deacon" or servant of all (CCE, 1997).[238] The doctrine of the diaconal "character" is consistent with the sacramentality of the diaconate and is a specific application to it of what Trent (1563) said of the sacrament of Holy Orders as a whole.[239] It rests on the witness of theological tradition.[240] It corroborates God's fidelity to his gifts, and implies the unrepeatable nature of the sacrament and lasting

stability in ecclesial service.[241] Finally, it confers upon the diaconate
a theological solidity that cannot be dissolved into something purely
functional. However, this doctrine does raise certain questions which
demand further theological clarifications. For instance, LG 10 lays
down that the distinction between the common priesthood of the
faithful and the ministerial priesthood is "essentia, non gradu tantum":
in what sense should this be applied to the diaconate?[242] While
maintaining the unity of the sacrament of Holy Orders, how should
the particularity of the diaconal character be further clarified in its
distinctive relation to the priestly character and the episcopal
character? What resources should be used to differentiate symbolically
the specific configuration with Christ of each of the three grades?

Vatican II does not use the vocabulary of configuration but
instead employs sober expressions which include sacramentality.[243] It
also speaks of a special share in the mission and grace of the Supreme
Priest.[244] In the Motu Proprio *Ad Pascendum* (1972) the permanent
deacon is considered a sign or sacrament of Christ himself.[245] The CCE
(1997) does make use of the vocabulary of configuration and links
it to the doctrine of character.[246] All these texts therefore give evidence
of a further development of the conciliar texts, starting from the
deacon's immediate relation with Christ by virtue of the sacrament
of Holy Orders. It only remains to describe its precise scope.

3. Diaconal action, "in persona Christi (Capitis)"?

The technical expression *"in persona Christi (Capitis)"* is used in
different ways in the texts of Vatican II. It is employed in reference to
the episcopal ministry, considered either as a whole or in one of the
functions proper to it;[247] particularly noticeable is its application to the
Eucharistic ministry of the ministerial priesthood (presbyterate) as
the maximum expression of this ministry,[248] because to preside at and
to consecrate the Eucharist belongs to its exclusive competence.[249]
The perspective is much wider in other texts, where the expression
may embrace the whole ministerial activity of the priest as a
personification of Christ the Head, or allude to other distinct specific
functions.[250] However, in the Conciliar texts there is no question
of applying this expression explicitly to the functions of the diaconal
ministry. Nevertheless, such a mode of expression does emerge in the
post-Conciliar documents.[251] That is currently a source of differences

of opinion on the part of theologians (especially in what concerns the representation of Christ the "Head"), because of the diverse meaning that the expression has in the documents of the Magisterium and in theological propositions.

If it is applied to the sacrament of Holy Orders as a whole, as being a specific participation in the threefold "munus" of Christ, then it can be said that the deacon also acts "in persona Christi (Capitis)" (or other equivalent expressions of a specific "representing" of Christ in the diaconal ministry), since the diaconate constitutes one of the grades of this sacrament. Today, many theologians follow this line, which is consistent with the sacramentality of the diaconate, and is supported by some documents of the Magisterium and certain theological trends. By contrast, those who reserve the expression to the functions of the priest alone, especially those of presiding at and consecrating the Eucharist, do not apply it to the diaconate and find corroboration of this opinion in the latest edition of the CCE (1997).

In the final edition of no. 875 of the CCE the expression "in persona Christi Capitis" is not applied to the diaconal functions of service.[252] In this case the capacity to act "in persona Christi Capitis" seems to be reserved to bishops and priests. Theological opinions are not unanimous on the question of whether this signifies a definitive exclusion or not. In a way, no. 875 of the CCE is a return to the language of LG 28a, PO 2c (priestly ministry) and LG 29a (triple diakonia). Furthermore, other texts from the CCE itself do seem to apply the expression to the whole of the sacrament of Holy Orders,[253] while recognizing a primordial role on the part of bishops and priests.[254] Thus there is a diversity of tendencies that are difficult to bring into harmony and which are clearly reflected in the various theological understandings of the diaconate. And even if it is considered theologically sound to understand the diaconal ministry as an action "in persona Christi (Capitis)," it still has to be clarified what characterizes the diaconate's specific way (the "specificum") of rendering Christ present as distinct from that of the episcopal ministry and the priestly ministry.

4. "In persona Christi Servi" as the specificity of the diaconate?

One way of doing this is to underline the aspect of "service" and see the specific characteristic, or a particularly distinctive element, of the diaconate, in the representation of the Christ the "Servant." This course appears in the most recent documents[255] and in some theological essays. However, difficulties arise, not because of the central importance of the notion of service for every ordained minister, but because this is made the specific criterion of the diaconal ministry. Could "headship" and "service" in the representating of Christ be separated so as to make each of the two a principle of specific differentiation? Christ the Lord is at the same time the supreme Servant and the servant of all.[256] The ministries of the bishop[257] and the priest, precisely in their function of presiding and of representing Christ the Head, Shepherd, and Spouse of his Church, also render Christ the Servant visible,[258] and require to be exercised as services. This is why it would seem problematic to aim to distinguish the diaconate through its exclusive representation of Christ as Servant. Given that service should be considered a characteristic common to every ordained minister,[259] the point in any case would be to see how in the diaconate it takes on predominant importance and particular solidity. To avoid disproportionate theological exchanges on this matter, it is appropriate to bear in mind simultaneously the unity of the person of Christ, the unity of the sacrament of order, and the symbolic character of the terms used to represent Christ ("head," "servant," "shepherd," "spouse").

5. Specific diaconal "functions"?

In Vatican II and the post-Conciliar documents, the functions attributed to deacons are many and diverse in varied fields, or, as LG 29a puts it, "in diaconia liturgiae, verbi et caritatis." These documents do not discuss the fact that all those tasks and functions can be carried out (as happens today in many communities) by Christians who have not received diaconal ordination. Now, according to AG 16f there do seem to exist "actual functions of the deacon's office" previous to ordination; and in this case ordination would merely strengthen, bind more closely to the altar, and make more effective because of the sacramental grace of the diaconate.[260] This statement confirms the doubts felt by some in regard to the sacramentality of the diaconate. How can this sacramentality be said to exist if it does not confer any specific "potestas" like that conferred by the priesthood and the episcopate? This same statement is taken by certain local churches as justifying mistrust and a negative attitude toward the institution of the permanent diaconate: why, they ask, proceed to this ordination if the same functions can be fulfilled by laypeople and lay ministers, who may be more effective and more adaptable? This theological matter thus has practical and pastoral repercussions which Vatican II did not deal with explicitly and which need to be tackled in the perspective of an ecclesiology of communion (cf. section IV. infra). The desire of the Council was to make it clear how each "potestas sacra" in the Church was rooted in the sacraments, and that was why the Council did not consider it indispensable to have recourse to the traditional distinction between "power of order" and "power of jurisdiction."[261] In any case that did not prevent it from reappearing in the post-Conciliar documents.[262]

III. THE DIACONATE IN THE PERSPECTIVE OF THE EPISCOPATE AS "PLENITUDO SACRAMENTI ORDINIS"

Vatican II gave a clear and authentic statement of the sacramentality of the episcopate, considering it as the "fullness of the sacrament of Orders" (LG 21b).[263] The reversal of views implied in this statement does not make the episcopal "fullness" any reason for depriving the priesthood and the diaconate of their proper consistency, as though their only meaning lay in being preparatory stages for the episcopate. In their participation in the one priesthood of Christ and the mission of salvation, priests cooperate with bishops and depend on them in the pastoral exercise of the ministry.[264] It now remains to see how the diaconate should be understood theologically from the same point of view.

1. The unity of the sacrament of Holy Orders

The statement of the unity of the sacrament of Holy Orders can be considered to form part of the common theological patrimony, and to have done so from the time (in the twelfth and following centuries) when the question was raised as to the sacramentality of the different degrees of Holy Orders.[265] This unity is maintained by Vatican II in speaking of the different orders, including the diaconate, in which the ecclesiastical ministry is exercised.[266] The post-Conciliar documents take the same line. The difficulties arise not from the assertion of this unity but from the theological path taken in order to justify it. Traditionally, this unity was justified by the relation of this sacrament to the Eucharist, while respecting the different modalities proper to each degree.[267] Vatican II modified the viewpoints and the formulations. Hence the need to seek another path to justify it. Such a path might well take as its starting point some consideration of the episcopate as the "fullness" of the sacrament of Holy Orders and the foundation of its unity.

2. "Profile" and "consistency" of the diaconate

There is a theological understanding of the ordained ministry perceived as "hierarchy," which has been preserved by Vatican II and in subsequent documents. This understanding[268] leads to the doctrine of the different "degrees" of Holy Orders. Here deacons represent the "lowest" degree in the hierarchical scale, in relation to bishops and priests.[269] The internal unity of the sacrament of Holy Orders means that each degree participates "suo modo" in the triple ministerial "munus," on a descending scale on which the higher degree includes and surpasses the whole reality and functions of the lower. This hierarchized and graded "participation" in one and the same sacrament means that the deacon is a minister who depends on the bishop and the priest.

The difficulty in giving the (permanent) diaconate its own profile and consistency in this hierarchized scheme of things has led to the proposal of other models of interpretation. It is obviously not compatible with the Conciliar texts to consider the episcopate, the priesthood, and the diaconate as three totally autonomous sacraments, juxtaposed and equal. The unity of the sacrament of Holy Orders would be seriously damaged, and such a view would prevent the episcopate from being seen as the "fullness" of the sacrament. For this reason certain contemporary theological approaches highlight the tradition of ancient sources and rites of ordination in which the diaconate appears "ad ministerium *episcopi*." The diaconate's direct and immediate relation to the episcopal ministry[270] would make deacons the natural collaborators of the bishop: that would imply for them the possibility of performing (preferentially) tasks in the superparochial and diocesan field.

In that case, what still remains to be explained more fully is the relation of the (permanent) diaconate with the priesthood. According to certain people, priests and deacons are on the same level with regard to the "fullness" of the sacrament represented by the episcopal ministry. Such people see this reflected in the ancient practice of ordinations (a deacon could be ordained bishop without necessarily passing through the priesthood, and a layman could be ordained a priest without passing through the diaconate[271]). These are historical facts that need to be borne in mind when delineating the ecclesiological profile of the diaconate today. However, it does not seem theologically justifiable to exclude deacons from every form of help and cooperation with priests,[272] and especially not with the "presbyterium" as a whole.[273] The hypothesis of a "diaconal college" around the bishop, as a manifestation of the "ordo diaconorum" similar to the "presbyterium"[274] and in communion with it, would require further theological study. The Conciliar and post-Conciliar texts say practically nothing about this possibility.[275] On the other hand, some contemporary theologico-pastoral essays maintain that the idea of a diaconal college would contribute solidity to the ecclesial profile required by a ministry that entails the demand of stability (the permanent diaconate).[276]

3. The imposition of hands "non ad sacerdotium . . ."

According to LG 29a, deacons receive the imposition of hands "non ad sacerdotium, sed ad ministerium." On this point Vatican II refers to text such as the *Statuta Ecclesiae Antiqua*,[277] whose formula has remained the same until our own times in the Roman Pontifical.[278] However, the formula goes back to the Traditio Apostolica (second through third centuries), that specifies something that is absent from the Council texts: "in ministerio episcopi."[279] Moreover, the interpretation of the precise meaning of this divergence is disputed in the current theology of the diaconate.[280] What seems excluded in this formulation ("sacerdotium") will be looked at first; after that, what seems to be stated in it (the relationship to "ministerium").

The diaconate is not "ad sacerdotium." How should this exclusion be interpreted? In a stricter sense the ministerial "sacerdotium" has been traditionally linked with the power "conficiendi eucharistiam,"[281] "offerendi sacrificium in Ecclesia,"[282] or "consecrandi verum corpus et sanguinem Domini."[283] Down the centuries, the basis for the sacramental equality of bishops and priests as "priests," i.e. those who offer sacrifice,[284] and the attribution of a solely jurisdictional origin to

the distinction between the two,[285] has been based on this close
connection between priesthood and Eucharist. This same reason, then,
is why deacons are not ordained "ad sacerdotium," given the impossibility
for them of presiding at and validly consecrating the Eucharist,
which is a power reserved exclusively to "priests." Does this restriction
also imply that the diaconate is excluded from "sacerdotium" understood in a less strict sense? Vatican II did indeed place the relationship
between the ministerial priesthood and the Eucharist in a wider
context: that of an ecclesiology centred on the Eucharist seen as *"totius
vitae christianae fons et culmen"*[286] and that of a ministerial priesthood
whose constitutive relationship with the Eucharist is rooted in a broader
"potestas sacra," also relating to the other ministerial *"munera."*[287] If
the diaconate is totally excluded from the "priesthood" in all senses
of the term, then it will be necessary to re-think the unity of the
sacrament of Holy Orders as "ministerial or hierarchical priesthood"
(cf. LG 10b), as well as the use of "sacerdotal" categories to make a
global definition or description of the sacrament. Different tendencies
are to be observed on this point in the Conciliar texts, in later
developments, and in theological studies of the diaconate.

On one hand the texts of Vatican II that explicitly mention
the diaconate do not apply terms or categories of priesthood to it, but
ministerial ones.[288] The same is true of the modifications introduced
for the sake of greater precision into the latest edition of the CCE,
which distinguishes clearly, within the single sacrament of Holy Orders,
between a degree of sacerdotal participation (episcopate and priesthood) and a degree of service (deacons), and which excludes the application of the term "sacerdos" to deacons.[289] On the other hand, when
Vatican II speaks from the perspective of the single sacrament of Holy
Orders, it seems to consider the "priestly" categories as all-inclusive
and extends them beyond the distinction between "sacerdotium" and
"ministerium." This is the case in LG 10b, which states that there
is a difference of essence and not merely of degree between the
common priesthood of the faithful and the ministerial or hierarchical
priesthood.[290] In the same way, when it speaks of the spirituality
of different states of life in LG 41d, the Council seems to attribute
an intermediate role to deacons in the collection of different ministries
(it should be noted that at that point the minor orders had not yet
been suppressed), by attributing to deacons a special share in the

mission and grace of the High Priest.[291] For its part, the 1983 CIC, in cann. 1008–9, includes deacons within the "sacri ministri," who by their consecration are enabled to pasture the People of God and to execute "pro suo quisque gradu" the functions of teaching, sanctifying, and ruling "in personal Christi Capitis."[292]

Because this was the state of affairs, it is not surprising to find that the post-Conciliar efforts to arrive at a theological understanding of the diaconate were marked by tensions born of whether the diaconate was excluded from or included in the priestly categories. As long as the diaconate was merely a step on the way to the priesthood, these tensions were manageable. From the moment when the diaconate was instituted as a permanent state and took shape and started to grow in many Churches,[293] the theological tensions became more pronounced and developed in two different directions.

On the basis of the unity of the sacrament of Holy Orders and in the conviction that they were being faithful to the Conciliar and post-Conciliar texts, some people stressed the unity of the sacrament and applied to the diaconate theological principles that were valid in proportionate ways for the three degrees of the sacrament. They maintained, with some differences of emphasis, that it should be generally understood and described as "sacerdotium ministeriale seu hierarchicum" (cf. LG 10b), which, they held, was borne out by the language used in the ancient tradition of the Church.[294] In this line of argument, the diaconate is a sacramental reality which implies a difference "essentia, non gradu tantum" (cf. LG 10b) in comparison with the common priesthood of the faithful. Hence the statement that the diaconate is "non ad sacerdotium" would then exclude only what related to the consecration of the Eucharist (and the sacrament of Reconciliation).[295] But both because of its integration within the single sacrament of Holy Orders, and because of its special relationship with the Eucharistic ministry, both by reason of the broadly "priestly" significance of the "munera" of teaching and government and by its specific participation in the mission and grace of the High Priest, the diaconate should still be included within the "ministerial or hierarchical priesthood," as distinct from the "common priesthood" of the faithful.

Other opposing tendencies insist strongly on the distinction expressed by the formula "non ad sacerdotium, sed ad ministerium."

In a line of argument contrary to that just outlined, these writers tend to exclude all "priestly" conceptualization or terminology from the correct understanding of the diaconate. At the same time they highlight this distinction as a decisive step toward overcoming the "sacerdotalization" of the sacrament of Holy Orders. They hold that this sacrament comprises three degrees, of which two (the episcopate and the priesthood) belong to the "sacerdotium" and one (the diaconate) is only "ad ministerium." In this way they avoid a theological understanding of the deacon in the image of a priest whose competencies are (still) limited. It would likewise enable a greater consistency and identity to be recognized in the deacon as a minister of the Church. However, the identity of the deacon is still to be defined in the light of LG 10b, because, as a sacramental reality, the diaconate is not to be identified with the functions, services, and ministries rooted in Baptism.

4. ". . . sed ad ministerium (episcopi)"

Certain theologico-pastoral studies of the (permanent) diaconate see the specific mention "in ministerio *episcopi*"[296] as a basis for asserting that the diaconate has a direct link with the Episcopal ministry.[297] While maintaining that this link does exist,[298] Vatican II softened the force it had in the *Traditio Apostolica* by stating that the diaconate was only "ad ministerium," in other words a service for the people exercised in the domain of the liturgy, the word, and charity, in communion with the bishop and his presbyterium.[299] John Paul II stressed this dimension of service to the People of God.[300] However, when it comes to specifying the theological scope of the expression "ad ministerium (episcopi)" and the possible integration of the diaconate into the ministry of apostolic succession, they return in a way to the divergences outlined above. Here too, the Conciliar and post-Conciliar texts are ambivalent.

In the light of LG 20 and 24a, it has been stated that the bishops are the successors of the apostles so as to prolong the first apostolic mission until the end of time.[301] As for LG 28a, it also seems to include deacons in the line of succession which prolongs the mission of Christ in that of the apostles, that of the bishops and that of the ecclesiastical ministry.[302] The CCE defines the sacrament of Holy Orders in its three degrees as "the sacrament of apostolic ministry."[303] With these texts as a basis, despite the variations in their terminology ("ecclesiastical" and "apostolic" ministry),[304] the diaconate could be considered as an integral part of the ministry of apostolic succession. This would fit in with the unity of the sacrament of Holy Orders, as rooted ultimately in Christ and with the deacons participating in their own way in the mission which the apostles and their successors received from Christ.[305]

However, this conclusion is not shared by those who retain the distinction between "sacerdotium" and "ministerium" as a difference of quality, and give decisive importance to the latest modifications to CCE no. 1154 (where the term "sacerdos" is reserved to bishops and priests). They see these modifications as going beyond what had been said up until that point, and as a key reference point for future developments. The apostolic ministry is understood as the continuation of the "diakonia" of Christ, which cannot be dissociated from his "priesthood": the priestly offering which he makes of his life actually constitutes his diaconal service for the salvation of the world. In this sense the "diakonia" or service characterizes the "munus" of the pastors (bishops) of the People of God[306] and it would not be sufficient to represent deacons as the specific heirs of the diaconal dimension of the ministry. The diaconate should be recognized as apostolic in its foundation, and not in its theological nature. That is to say, therefore, that the ministry of apostolic succession should be restricted to "priests"[307] (bishops and priests), while deacons would form part of the "ecclesiastical" ministry[308] and should be considered, consequently, as auxiliary collaborators toward the ministry of apostolic succession, and not, strictly speaking, an integral part of it.

5. The diaconate as mediating function or "medius ordo"?

The interventions made at the Council, and the notes of the relevant Conciliar Commission, already attributed to the permanent diaconate a mediating or bridging function between the hierarchy and the people.[309] Although this idea was not retained in the definitive Council texts, it was in a way reflected in the order adopted in LG 29: the text speaks of deacons at the end of Chapter III as the last degree of the hierarchy, just before dealing with the subject of laypeople in Chapter IV. The same order is found in AG 16. The actual expression "medius ordo" applied explicitly to the (permanent) diaconate is found only in the Motu Proprio *Ad Pascendum* (1972) and is presented as one way of putting into effect the hopes and intentions that had led Vatican II to restore it.[310] The idea spread widely in contemporary theology, and gave rise to different ways of conceiving this mediating function: between clergy and laity, between the Church and the world, between worship and ordinary life, between charity work and the Eucharist, between the center and the periphery of the Christian community. Whatever the context, the notion merits some theological clarifications.

It would be a theological error to identify the diaconate as "medius ordo" with a kind of intermediate (sacramental?) reality between the baptized and the ordained faithful. The fact that the diaconate belongs to the sacrament of Holy Orders is sure doctrine. Theologically the deacon is not a "layperson." Vatican II considers that the deacon is a member of the hierarchy and the CIC refers to him as "sacer minister" or "clericus."[311] It is true that it belongs to the deacon to accomplish some sort of task of mediation, but it would not be theologically correct to make that task into the expression of the diaconate's theological nature or its specifying note. Additionally, there is a certain risk that the fixing of the diaconate in ecclesiological terms, and institutionalizing it in pastoral terms as "medius ordo" might end up by sanctioning and deepening, through that very function, the gap that it was supposed to fill.

These theological clarifications do not imply a total rejection of all mediating function on the part of the deacon. The notion is based on the witnesses of ecclesial tradition.[312] In a certain way it is reflected in the ecclesiological position which current canon law (CIC 1983) attributes to deacons between the mission of laypeople and that of priests. On the one hand, (permanent) deacons live in the middle of the world with a lay style of life (although there is the possibility of a religious permanent diaconate) and with certain "concessions" which are not (or not always) accorded to all clergy and priests.[313] On the other hand there are certain functions in which deacons and priests share alike, and in which both alike take precedence over the laity.[314] That does not mean that deacons can exercise completely all the functions that belong to priests (Eucharist, Reconciliation, Anointing of the Sick). However, except in certain exceptional cases, what the CIC lays down for "clergy" in general is, in principle, applied to deacons (cf. can. 273 ff.).

IV. The Diaconate in an "Ecclesiology of Communion"

Although it is based on the texts of Vatican II, what can be called the "ecclesiology of communion" was developed in greater depth in and after the synod of 1985.[315] This ecclesiology grants a clearer understanding of the Church as a "universal sacrament of salvation" (cf. LG 1, 9) which finds in the communion of the Trinitarian God the source and ecclesial model for all the dynamism of salvation. "Diakonia" is the realization of this model in history. It now remains to be seen how the specific sacramental configuration of the diaconal ministry is integrated within this "diakonia" as a whole.

1. The "munera" of the diaconate: plurality of functions and varying priorities

LG 29a lists and explains the diaconal functions in the field of the liturgy (which includes tasks where the deacons presides), of the word, and of charity, to which administrative tasks are connected.[316] AG 16f follows another order: ministry of the word, of the government of communities, and of charity.[317] For its part, *Sacrum Diaconatus* singles out eleven tasks, eight of which belong to the liturgical sphere (which is given first rank in this way) although sometimes they have the character of "supply" tasks. The charitable and social work is done in the name of the hierarchy, and also includes the duty of stimulating the lay apostolate.[318] The CIC goes into details on the faculties and tasks that properly belong to deacons; the possibility is there mentioned of conferring on deacons a share in the exercise of the "cura pastoralis" of the parish.[319] With reference to the Conciliar texts of LG 29, SC 35, and AG 16, the CCE takes up the familiar list of relationships to liturgical life (with an explicit mention of assistance to bishops and priests), to pastoral life, and to charitable and social works.[320] The *Ratio Fundamentalis* presents the diaconal ministry as an exercise of the three "munera" in the specific light of "diakonia," enumerated as the "munus docendi," the "munus sanctificandi" (with the Eucharist as its point of departure and its destination), and the "munus regendi" (where charitable activities are given as the most characteristic ministry of the deacon).[321] And the *Directorium* takes up again the triple diakonia of LG 29, though changing the order (word, liturgy, charity). In this way it retains the diakonia of the word as the main function of the deacon; it underlines the diakonia of the liturgy as an intrinsic and organic assistance to the priestly ministry, and it considers the diakonia of charity as a different way of participating in the pastoral tasks of the bishops and priests.[322]

The different functions attributed to the (permanent) diaconate in the Conciliar and post-Conciliar texts general come down to us from ancient liturgical tradition, from the rites of ordination and theological studies of them. These functions are also open to contemporary pastoral situations and needs, although in that case a certain reserve is noticeable in the documents. In general a sort of triple "diakonia" or a sort of triple "munus" is recognized and serves as the basis for the diaconal functions taken together. In the documents and in numerous theological studies, charitable works are given a certain pre-eminence;[323] however, it would be problematic to consider these as being specific to the diaconate, because they are also properly the responsibility of the bishops and the priests, whose auxiliaries the deacons are. Moreover, the witness of ecclesial tradition suggest that the three functions ought to be integrated into a single whole. From that point of view, it is possible to point out different characteristic features in the figure of the diaconal ministry. This ministry may be more strongly focused either on charity, or on the liturgy, or on evangelization; it may be exercised in a service directly linked to the bishop, or else in the sphere of the parish; and the permanent diaconate and the transitory diaconate may be preserved alike, or a clear option for one single figure may be determined. How plausible, and how viable, would such diversity prove to be in the long term? That would depend not only on the way the diaconate is understood theologically, but also on the real situation of different local churches.

2. Communion in a plurality of ministries

The specific way the diaconate is exercised in different surroundings will also help to define its ministerial identity, modifying if necessary an ecclesial framework in which its proper connection with the ministry of the bishop hardly appears and in which the figure of the priest is identified with the totality of the ministerial functions.

The living consciousness that the Church is "communion" will contribute to this development. However, it would be hard to arrive at a solution to the theological queries about the specific "powers" of the diaconate through practical experience alone. Not everyone considers this question to be an insoluble difficulty. Thus different propositions of contemporary theology may be observed which aim to give the diaconate theological substance, ecclesial acceptance, and pastoral credibility.

There are some people who consider that this question of the "powers" of the deacon to have only relative importance. For them, to make it into a central question would be a kind of reductionism and would disfigure the true meaning of the ordained minister. Moreover, the observation, which was true in ancient times as well, that a layman can exercise the tasks of the deacon did not in practice prevent this ministry from being considered sacramental from every point of view. Additionally, neither would it be possible to reserve the exclusive exercise of certain functions to bishops and priests in great detail, save in the case of the "potestas conficiendi eucharistiam,"[324] of the sacrament of Reconciliation[325] and the ordination of bishops.[326] Other people distinguish between what is or should be the normal and ordinary exercise of the whole collection of functions attributed to deacons, and what could be considered as an extraordinary exercise of them on the part of Christians,[327] determined by pastoral needs or emergencies, even on a long-term basis. A certain analogy could be drawn between this and the normal or ordinary competencies of the bishop in regard to confirmation (which the priest can also administer)[328] and in regard to the ordination of priests (which according to certain papal bulls seems to have been performed by priests too in exceptional cases).[329]

Finally, there are some who also throw doubt on whether in fact a nonordained member of the faithful does perform exactly the same "munera" in the same way and with the same salvific effect as an ordained deacon.[330] Even if they seem to be the same functions as are exercised by a nonordained member of the faithful, the deciding factor would be what the deacon *was* rather than what he *did:* the action of the deacon would bring about a special presence of Christ the Head and Servant that was proper to sacramental grace, configuration with Him, and the community and public dimension of the tasks that are carried out in the name of the Church. The viewpoint of faith and the sacramental reality of the diaconate would enable its particular distinctiveness to be discovered and affirmed, not in relation to its functions but in relation to its theological nature and its representative symbolism.

V. Conclusion

From the point of view of its theological meaning and its ecclesial role the ministry of the diaconate presents a challenge to the Church's awareness and practice, particularly through the questions that it still raises today. With reference to deacons, plenty of witnesses from Tradition recall that the Lord chose acts of humble service to express and render present the reality of the *morphe doulou* (Philippians 2:7) which he assumed for the sake of his saving mission. Specifically, the diaconate was born as a help to the apostles and their successors, who were themselves perceived as servants of Christ. If the diaconate has been restored as a permanent ministry by Vatican II it is especially to respond to specific needs (cf. LG 29b) or to grant sacramental grace to those who were already carrying out the functions of the deacon's office (AG 16f). But the task of identifying these needs and these functions more clearly in Christian communities is still to be done, although the rich experience of the particular Churches which, after the Council, gave the permanent diaconate a place in their pastoral practice, is already available.

In the current consciousness of the Church, there is only one single sacrament of Holy Orders. Vatican II, taking up the teaching of Pius XII,[331] affirmed this unity and saw the episcopate, the priesthood and the diaconate as included within it. According to the decision of Paul VI, it is only these three ordained ministries that constitute the clerical state.[332] However, concerning the diaconate the Council cautiously speaks only of "sacramental grace." After Vatican II, Paul VI[333] and the CCE (no. 1570) teach that the deacon, through ordination, receives the character of the sacrament of Holy Orders. Can. 1008 of the CIC states that the three ordained ministries are exercised *in persona Christi Capitis*.[334] Following LG 29, which attributed to the deacon the solemn administration of Baptism (cf. SC 68), can. 861, 1 spoke of each of the three ordained ministers as ordinary ministers of this sacrament; can. 129 recognized that the *potestas regiminis* belonged to all those who have received the sacrament of Holy Orders.[335]

On the other hand, the difference between the sacerdotal ministries and the diaconal ministry is also underlined. The Council statement that the deacon is not ordained for priesthood but for ministry was taken up by various documents of the post-Conciliar Magisterium. Most clearly of all, the CCE (no. 154) distinguishes within one and the same *ordinatio*, the *gradus participationis sacerdotalis* of the episcopate and the priesthood, and the *gradus servitii* of the diaconate. The diaconate, by the very nature of its *way of participating* in the one mission of Christ, carries out this mission in the manner of an auxiliary service. It is *"icona vivens Christi servi in Ecclesia,"* but, precisely as such, it maintains a constitutive link with the priestly ministry to which it lends its aid (cf. LG 41). It is not just any service that is attributed to the deacon in the Church: his service belongs to the sacrament of Holy Orders, as a close collaboration with the bishop and the priests, in the unity of the same ministerial actualization of the mission of Christ. The CCE (no. 1554) quotes Saint Ignatius of Antioch: "Let everyone revere the deacons as Jesus Christ, the bishop as the image of the Father, and the presbyters as the senate of God and the assembly of the apostles. For without them one cannot speak of the Church."[336]

With regard to the ordination of women to the diaconate, it should be noted that two important indications emerge from what has been said up to this point:

(1) The deaconesses mentioned in the tradition of the ancient church—as evidenced by the rite of institution and the functions they exercised—were not purely and simply equivalent to the deacons;

(2) The unity of the sacrament of Holy Orders, in the clear distinction between the ministries of the Bishop and the Priests on the one hand and the Diaconal ministry on the other, is strongly under-lined by ecclesial tradition, especially in the teaching of the magisterium.

In the light of these elements which have been set out in the present historico-theological research document, it pertains to the ministry of discernment which the Lord established in his Church to pronounce authoritatively on this question.

Over and above all the questions raised by the diaconate, it is good to recall that ever since Vatican II the active presence of this ministry in the life of the Church has aroused, in memory of the example of Christ, a more vivid awareness of the value of service for Christian life.

---

229. Cf. AAS 59 (1967) 697–704; AAS 60 (1968) 369–373; AAS 64 (1973) 534–540; *Codex Iuris Canonici,* Città del Vaticano 1983; *Catechismus Catholicae Ecclesiae,* Città del Vaticano 1997.

230. This is the case of two recent guidance documents: Congregatio De Institutione Catholica/Congregatio Pro Clericis, *Ratio fundamentalis institutionis diaconorum permanentium. Directorium pro ministerio et vita diaconorum permanentium,* Città del Vaticano 1998. According to Cardinal Pio Laghi, the *Ratio Fundamentalis* is a document "di ordine eminentemente pedagogico e non dottrinale" and, according to Cardinal Darìo Castrillón, the *Directorium* "intende presentare linee pratiche." *Oss. Rom.* 11.03.1998, pp. 6–7.

231. "Christus, 'sedens ad dexteram Patris' et Spiritum Sanctum in Suum effundens corpus, quod est Ecclesia, iam operatur per sacramenta a Se instituta ad Suam gratiam communicandam . . . Efficaciter gratiam efficient quam significant propter Christi actionem et per Spiritus Sancti virtutem," CCE no. 1084.

232. "Sunt efficacia quia in eis Ipse Christus operatur: Ipse est qui baptizat, Ipse est qui in Suis agit sacramentis ut gratiam communicet quam sacramentum significat . . . Hic est sensus affirmationis Ecclesiae: sacramenta agunt ex opere operato . . . , i.e., virtute salvifici operis Christi, semel pro semper adimpleti," CCE nos. 1127f.

233. Cf. CCE no. 1536: "Ordo est sacramentum per quod missio a Christo Ipsius Apostolis concredita exerceri pergit in Ecclesia usque ad finem temporum: est igitur ministerii apostolici sacramentum. Tres implicat gradus: Episcopatum, presbyteratum et diaconatum."

234. For the application of the passage about the washing of the feet to deacons, cf. *Didascalia* XVI, 13 (trans. F. Nau, Paris 1912, 135f.) and H. Wasserschleben, *Die irische Canonensammlung,* Leipzig 1885, 26: "diaconus (fuit) Christus, quando lavit pedes discipulorum," cf. K. Rahner–H. Vorgrimmler, *Diaconia in Christo,* Freiburg 1962, 104. Recently, W. Kasper proposed seeing in the washing of the feet and in the words of Jesus at John 13:15 "die Stiftung des Diakonats," *Der Diakon in ekklesiologischer Sicht angesichts der gegenwärtigen Herausforderungen in Kirche und Gesellschaft,* in: *Diaconia in*

Christo 32/3–4 (1997) 22. In reality it is the whole of the passage at Mark 10:43–45 that *Didascalia* III, 13 cites in relation to deacons. For his part, Saint Ignatius of Antioch considers that deacons were entrusted with "the service of Jesus Christ" (*Magn.* 6, 1) and Saint Polycarp exhorts them to walk in the truth of the Lord, who became the "diakonos" of all (*Philippians* 5:2).

235. Current exegetical debate on the consideration of Acts of the Apostles 6:1–6 as the origin of the diaconate goes back to the Patristic texts: Saint Irenaeus (second century), AH I, 26, 3; III, 12, 10 sees the ordination of the "Seven" as the beginning of the diaconate; Saint John Chrysostom (circa 400), *In Acta Apost.* 14, 3 (PG 60, 115f.) does not consider the "Seven" to be deacons, although he does interpret their post as an ordination and a share in the apostolic mission. This second opinion was adopted by the synod In Trullo (690), a synod which has the status of an ecumenical council for the Orthodox Church, cf. Conc. Quinisextum, can. 16, (Mansi 11, 949; ed. Ioannou, I/1, 132–134).

236. The differentiation into three grades or degrees appears clearly in the post-apostolic period, first perhaps with Saint Ignatius of Antioch's *Ad Trall.* 3,1. On this question, cf. E. Dassmann, *Ämter und Dienste in der frühchristlichen Gemeinden*, Bonn 1994; E. Cattaneo, *I ministeri della Chiesa antica. Testi patristici dei primi tre secoli,* Milan 1997.

237. "Sic ministerium ecclesiasticum divinitus institutum diversis ordinibus exercetur ab illis qui iam ab antiquo Episcopi, Presbyteri, Diaconi vocantur," LG 28a; with references to Trent, DS 1765 (". . . in Ecclesiae ordinatissima dispositione plures et diversi essent ministrorum ordines... ab ipso Ecclesiae initio . . .") and DS 1776 (". . . hierarchiam, divina ordinatione institutam, quae constat ex episcopis, presbyteris et ministris . . .").

238. "non tamquam merus ad sacerdotium gradus est existimandus, sed indelebile suo charactere ac praecipua sua gratia insignis ita locupletatur, ut qui ad ipsum vocentur, ii mysteriis Christi et Ecclesiae stabiliter inservire possint," Paul VI, *Sacrum Diaconatus,* AAS 59 (1967), 698. "Diaconi missionem et gratiam Christi, modo speciali, participant. Ordinis sacramentum eos signat *sigillo* ('charactere') quod nemo delere potest et quod eos configurat Christo qui factus est 'diaconus', id est, omnium minister," CCE no. 1570. "Prout gradus Ordinis sacri, diaconatus characterem imprimit et specificam gratiam sacramentalem communicat. Character diaconalis est signum configurativum-distinctivum animae modo indelebili impressum . . .," *Ratio Fundamentalis,* no. 7. In the measure in which can. 1008 of the CIC also refers to the diaconate, its indelible character may also be considered to be stated there.

239. "Quoniam vero in sacramento ordinis, sicut et in baptismo et confirmatione, character imprimitur, qui nec deleri nec auferri potest: merito sancta Synodus damnat eorum sententiam, qui asserunt, Novi Testamenti

sacerdotes temporariam tantummodo potestatem habere, et semel rite ordinatos iterum laicos effici posse, si verbi Dei ministerium non exerceant." Council of Trent, DS 1767.

240. Cf. Saint Thomas, *In IV Sent.* d 7 q 2 ad 1; *STh* III q 63 a 3.

241. Although it does not specifically mention the doctrine of "character," as regards the diaconate the *Directorium* states (no. 21): "Sacra Ordinatio, semel valide recepta, numquam evanescit. Amissio tamen status clericalis fit iuxta normas iure canonico statutas."

242. The *Directorium* (no. 28) speaks of the "essential difference" that exists between the ministry of the deacon at the altar and that of every other liturgical minister; however, it gives a reference not to LG 10, but to LG 29: "Constat eius diaconiam apud altare, quatenus a sacramento Ordinis effectam, essentialiter differre a quolibet ministerio liturgico, quod pastores committere possint christifidelibus non ordinatis. Ministerium liturgicum diaconi pariter differt ab ipso ministerio sacerdotali."

243. ". . . gratia sacramentali roborati," LG 29a; ." . . gratiam sacramentalem diaconatus," AG 16f.

244. "Missionis autem et gratiae supremi Sacerdotis peculiari modo participes sunt inferioris quoque ordinis ministri, imprimis Diaconi, qui mysteriis Christi et Ecclesiae servientes . . ." LG 41d.

245. ." . . Diaconatus permanens . . . signum vel sacramentum ipsius Christi Domini, qui non venit ministrari, sed ministrare," Paul VI, *Ad Pascendum*, AAS 54 (1972) 536.

246. In reference to LG 41 and AG 16, the CCE says (no. 1570): "Diaconi missionem et gratiam Christi, modo speciali, participant. Ordinis sacramentum eos signat *sigillo* ('charactere') quod nemo delere potest et quod eos configurat Christo qui factus est 'diaconus', id est, omnium minister." Meanwhile the *Ratio* (nos. 5, 7) links this configuration to the outpouring of the Spirit and identifies it specifically by its assimilation to Christ as Servant of all: "Diaconatus confertur per peculiarem effusionem Spiritus (*ordinatio*), quae in recipientis persona specificam efficit configurationem cum Christo, Domino et Servo omnium . . . is (diaconus) enim, prout unici ministerii ecclesiastici particeps, est in Ecclesia specificum signum sacramentale Christi servi . . . Character diaconalis est signum configurativum-distinctivum animae modo indelebili impressum, quod sacro ordine auctos configurat Christo . . ."

247. The sacramentality of the episcopate implies that "Episcopi, eminenti ac adspectabili modo, ipsius Christi Magistri, Pastoris et Pontificis partes sustineant et in Eius persona agant," LG 21b; at other points analogous formulas are used such as: "Episcopi sententiam de fide et moribus nomine Christi prolatam," LG 25; "potestas qua, nomine Christi, personaliter funguntur," LG 27; "munus in ipsius nomine et potestate docendi, sanctificandi et regendi," AA 2b; "oves suas in nomine Domini pascunt," CD 11b.

248. In LG 10b, on the subject of the essential difference between the common priesthood of the faithful and the ministerial priesthood, it is said of the ministerial priesthood that "potestate sacra, qua gaudet, populum sacerdotalem efformat ac regit, sacrificium eucharisticum in persona Christi conficit illudque nomine totius populi Deo offert"; in turn, LG 28a states of priests that "suum verum munus sacrum maxime exercent in eucharistico cultu vel synaxi, qua in persona Christi agentes . . . unicum sacrificium . . . repraesentant"; likewise PO 13b states that "praesertim in sacrificio Missae, presbyteri personam specialiter gerunt Christi."

249. The connection of "in persona Christi" with the exclusive competence of the priest to consecrate the Eucharist was underlined in the post-Conciliar documents: the synod of 1971 stated that "solus sacerdos in persona Christi agere valet ad praesidendum et perficiendum sacrificale convivium," *Ench. Vat.* IV 1166; the letter of the Congregation for the Doctrine of the Faith, *Sacerdotium ministeriale*, 1983, stresses that "munus tam grave conficiendi mysterium eucharisticum adimplere valeant (episcopi et presbyteri) . . . ut ipsi . . . non communitatis mandato, sed agant in persona Christi," AAS 75 (1983) 1006; this is recalled in the 1983 CIC: "Minister, qui in persona Christi sacramentum Eucharistiae conficere valet, est solus sacerdos valide ordinatus," can. 900, 1.

250. "Presbyteri, unctione Spiritus Sancti, speciali charactere signantur et sic Christo Sacerdoti configurantur, ita ut in persona Christi Capitis agere valeant," PO 2c; the equivalent expression in PO 12a goes in the same direction: ". . . omnis sacerdos, suo modo, ipsius Christi personam gerat." The priestly ministry as a whole is included in the references of AG 39a ("Presbyteri personam Christi gerunt... in triplice sacro munere . . .") and LG 37a (". . . illos, qui ratione sacri sui muneris personam Christi gerunt"); in SC 33a it is made more specific as a presiding at the celebration of the Eucharist: "Immo preces a sacerdote, qui coetui in persona Christi praeest, . . . dicuntur." Post-Conciliar documents: in *Evangelii Nuntiandi*, Paul VI applies the formula to the ministry of evangelization: "Cum Episcopis in ministerium evangelizationis consocientur . . . ii qui per sacerdotalem ordinationem personam Christi gerunt," EN 67, *Ench. Vat.* V, 1683; John Paul II employs it when referring to the specific ministry of reconciliation in the sacrament of penance: "Sacerdos, Paenitentiae minister . . . agit in persona Christi," *Reconc. et Paenit.* (1984) no. 29; according to *Pastores Dabo Vobis* (1992), the priest represents Christ the Head, Shepherd and Spouse of the Church: ". . . connectuntur cum 'consecratione', quae eorum propria est eosque ad Christum, Ecclesiae Caput et Pastorem configurat; vel cum 'missione' vel ministerio presbyterorum proprio, quod eos habiles efficit et instruit ut fiant 'Christi Sacerdotis aeterni viva instrumenta' et ad agendum provehit 'Ipsius

Christi nomine et persona' . . .," no. 20; "Presbyter, per sacramentalem hanc consecrationem, configuratur Christo Iesu quatenus Capiti et Pastori Ecclesiae . . .," no. 21; "Sacerdos ergo advocatur ut sit imago vivens Iesu Christi, Ecclesiae sponsi: remanet ipse quidem semper communitatis pars . . . , sed vi eiusdem configurationis ad Christum Caput et Pastorem, ipse presbyter positus est in eiusmodi relatione sponsali erga propriam communitatem," no. 22.

251. The 1983 CIC applies the formula to the whole of the sacrament of Holy Orders, and consequently to the diaconate as well: "Sacramento ordinis . . . consecrantur et deputantur ut, pro suo quisque gradu, in persona Christi Capitis munera docendi, sanctificandi et regendi adimplendi, Dei populum pascant. Ordines sunt episcopatus, presbyteratus et diaconatus," can. 1008/9. An intervention by John Paul II includes the idea of personification, but applied to Christ the servant, cf. note 255 *infra*. The 1998 *Directorium* prefers the formula "in the name of Christ" to refer to the Eucharistic ministry of the deacon ("nomine ipsius Christi, inservit ad Ecclesiam participem reddendam fructuum sacrificii sui," no. 28) and in relation with the diakonia of charity ("Vi sacramenti Ordinis diaconus . . . munera pastoralia participat . . . quae participatio, utpote per sacramentum peracta, efficit ut diaconi Populum Dei inserviant nominee Christi," no. 37).

252. "Ab Eo (Christo) Episcopi et presbyteri missionem et facultatem ('sacram potestatem') agendi *in persona Christi Capitis* accipiunt, diaconi vero vim populo Dei serviendi in 'diaconia' liturgiae, verbi et caritatis . . ." CCE no. 875.

253. "Per ordinationem recipitur capacitas agendi tamquam Christi legatus, Capitis Ecclesiae . . ." CCE no. 1581; ." . . sacramento ordinis, cuius munus est, nomine et in persona Christi Capitis, in communitate servire," CCE no. 1591; "In ecclesiali ministri ordinati servitio, Ipse Christus, Ecclesiae suae est praesens, quatenus Caput Sui corporis . . ." CCE no. 1548.

254. "Per ministerium ordinatum, prasertim Episcoporum et presbyterorum, praesentia Christi, tamquam Capitis Ecclesiae, in communitate credentium, visibilis fit," CCE no. 1549.

255. For example, the *Ratio Fundamentalis* stresses the simultaneous configuration of the deacon "cum Christo, Domino et Servo omnium" and considers it to be "specificum signum sacramentale Christi Servi," no. 5. John Paul II, for his part, stated (16 March 1985): "Il diacono nel suo grado personifica Cristo servo del Padre, partecipando alla triplice funzione del sacramento dell' Ordine," *Insegnamenti* VIII/1, 649.

256. The same text of Saint Polycarp, *Ad Phil.* 5, 2 (ed. Funk I, 300), which LG 29a and the *Ratio* no. 5 apply to deacons, considers Christ as Lord and Servant (minister): "Misericordes, seduli, incedentes iuxta veritatem Domini, qui omnium minister factus est."

257. On the subject of bishops, LG 24a declares: "Munus autem illud, quod Dominus pastoribus populi sui commisit, verum est servitium quod in sacris Litteris *diakonia* seu ministerium significanter nuncupatur (cf. Acts of the Apostles 1:17 and 25; 21:19; Romans 11:13; 1 Timothy 1:12)."

258. Cf. *Pastores Dabo Vobis*, no. 21: "Christus est Ecclesiae Caput, sui scilicet Corporis. 'Caput' est eo modo quidem novo et sibi proprio modo, 'servum' scilicet significandi, prout ab Ipsius verbis evincitur (Mark 10:45) . . . Quod servitium seu 'ministerium' plenitudinem sui attigit per mortem in cruce acceptam, id est per totale sui donum, in humilitate at amore (Philippians 2:7–8) . . . Auctoritas autem Christi Iesu Capitis eadem est ac Ipsius servitium, donum, totalis deditio, humilis atque dilectionis plena, erga Ecclesiam. Idque in perfecta erga Patrem obedientia. Ille enim, unicus verusque est afflictus et dolens Domini Servus, idemque Sacerdos et Hostia seu Victima."

259. CCE states (no. 876): "Intrinsece coniuncta naturae sacramentali ministerii ecclesialis est *eius indoles servitii.* Ministri etenim, prorsus dependentes a Christo qui missionem praebet et auctoritatem, vere sunt 'servi Christi' ad imaginem Christi qui libere propter nos 'formam servi' (Philippians 2:7) accepit. Quia verbum et gratia quorum sunt ministri, eorum non sunt, sed Christi qui illa eis pro aliis concredidit, ipsi libere omnium fient servi."

260. "Iuvat enim viros, qui ministerio vere diaconali fungantur . . . per impositionem manuum inde ab Apostolis traditam corroborari et altari arctius coniungi, ut ministerium suum per gratiam sacramentalem diaconatus efficacius expleant." AG 16f.

261. Vatican II does not use the expression "potestas iurisdictionis" and only in PO 2b does it speak of "sacra ordinis potestas." However, in the *Explanatory Note,* no. 2, of LG, it affirms with reference to Episcopal consecration: "In consecratione datur ontologica participatio sacrorum munerum, ut indubie constat ex Traditione, etiam liturgica. Consulto adhibetur vocabulum munerum, non vero potestatum, quia haec ultima vox de potestate ad actum expedita intelligi posset. Ut vero talis expedita potestas habeatur, accedere debet canonica seu iuridica determinatio per auctoritatem hierarchicam. Quae determinatio potestatis consistere potest in concessione particularis officii vel in assignatione subditorum, et datur iuxta normas a suprema auctoritate adprobatas. Huiusmodi ulterior norma ex natura rei requiritur, quia agitur de muneribus quae a pluribus subiectis, hierarchice ex voluntate Christi cooperantibus, exerceri debent." On the different interpretations of the "potestas sacra," cf. Krämer, *Dienst und Vollmacht in der Kirche. Eine rechtstheologische Untersuchung zur Sacra Potestas-Lehre des II. Vatikanischen Konzils,* Trier 1973, 38f.; A. Celeghin, *Origine e natura della potestà sacra. Posizioni postconciliari,* Brescia 1987.

262. CIC, can. 966, distinguishes between "potestate ordinis" and "facultate eandem exercendi."

263. "Docet autem Sancta Synodus episcopali consecratione plenitudinem conferri sacramenti Ordinis, quae nimirum et liturgica Ecclesiae consuetudine et voce sanctorum Patrum summum sacerdotium, sacri ministerii summa nuncupatur," LG 21b. The doctrinal *relatio* understands the expression finally used (plenitudo sacramenti) as "totalitas omnis partes includens," AS III/I, 238. LG 41b considers bishops to be "ad imaginem summi et aeterni Sacerdotis, Pastoris et Episcopi . . . ad plenitudinem sacerdotii electi."

264. "Presbyteri, quamvis pontificatus apicem non habeant et in exercenda sua potestate ab Episcopis pendeant, cum eis tamen sacerdotali honore coniuncti sunt et vi sacramenti Ordinis, ad imaginem Christi, summi atque aeterni Sacerdotis . . . consecrantur, ut veri sacerdotes Novi Testamenti. Muneris unici Mediatoris Christi (1 Timothy 2:5) participes in suo gradu ministerii . . . Presbyteri, ordinis Episcopalis provide cooperatores eiusque adiutorium . . ." LG 28.

265. Cf. several references in L. Ott, *Das Weihesakrament* (HbDG IV/5), Freiburg 1969. Trent, cf. DS 1763–1778, takes its unity for granted as a starting-point when speaking of the "sacrament of Order," as in the case of Baptism and Confirmation (cf. DS 1767).

266. "Sic ministerium ecclesiasticum divinitus institutum diversis ordinibus exercetur ab illis qui iam ab antiquo episcopi, presbyteri, diaconi vocantur," LG 28a.

267. Cf. Saint Thomas, *STh*, III, *Suppl.* q37 a2 Resp.: ." . . distinctio ordinis est accipienda secundum relationem ad Eucharistiam. Quia potestas ordinis aut est ad consecrationem Eucharistiae ipsius, aut ad aliquod ministerium ordinandum ad hoc. Si primo modo, sic est ordo sacerdotum . . ."

268. Cf. LG 10b: "sacerdotium ministeriale seu hierarchicum;" the CCE gives the heading "Hierarchica Ecclesiae constitutio" to the doctrine on the ecclesial ministry which it sets out in nos. 874–896.

269. "In gradu inferiori hierarchiae sistunt Diaconi," LG 29a. With the suppression of the other degrees in *Ministeria quaedam* (1972), the diaconate became in fact the last degree.

270. The *Directorium* (no. 8) speaks explicitly of "participation" in the episcopal ministry: "Fundamentum obligationis consistit in ipsa participatione ministerii episcopalis, quae per sacramentum Ordinis et missionem canonicam confertur." Further on, no. 11 warns against what would prejudice the "relation directa et inmediata, quam quilibet diaconus cum proprio episcopo habere debet."

271. Cf. M. Andrieu, *La carrière ecclésiastique des papes et les documents liturgiques du Moyen-Âge*, in: Rev Sc Rel 21 (1947) 90–120.

272. In regard to their relation with bishops, the *Ratio Fundamentalis* (1998), no. 8, says that deacons "depend" on bishops in the exercise of their power; and speaks of a "special relationship" of deacons with priests: "Diaconi, cum ecclesiasticum ministerium in inferiore gradu participent, in sua potestate exercenda necessario ex Episcopis pendent prout plenitudinem sacramenti habentibus. Praeterea, necessitudinem peculiarem cum presbyteris ineunt, quippe in communione quorum ad populum Dei serviendum sunt vocati."

273. ". . . (Diaconi) Populo Dei, in communione cum Episcopo eiusque *presbyterio,* inserviunt," LG 29a. The Motu Proprio *Sacrum Diaconatus* no. 23, which applies the Conciliar decisions, underlines submission to the authority of the bishop and the priest: "Quae omnia munera in perfecta cum episcopo eiusque presbyterio communione exsequenda sunt, videlicet sub auctoritate episcopi et presbyteri, qui eo loci fidelium curae praesunt:" The *Caeremoniale Episcoporum* . . . , Typ. Pol. Vat. 1985, no. 24 says with regard to deacons: "Spiritus Sancti dono roborati, Episcopo eiusque *presbyterio* adiumentum praestant in ministerio verbi, altaris et caritatis."

274. Deacons cannot be members of the council of priests; cf. LG 28, CD 27, PO 7, CIC can. 495, 1. This is confirmed by the *Directorium,* no. 42: "Nequeunt tamen esse membra consilii presbyteralis, quia ipsum exclusive presbyterium repraesentat."

275. The 1998 *Directorium* (no. 6) recalls the "sacramental fraternity" which unites deacons, the importance of the bonds of charity, prayer, unity, and cooperation, and that it is opportune for them to meet together; but it says nothing about the possibility of a collegial "ordo diaconorum," and it warns against the risks of "corporatism" which was a factor in the disappearance of the permanent diaconate in earlier centuries: "Diaconi, vi ordinis accepti, fraternitate sacramentali inter se uniti sunt . . . Praestat ut diaconi, consentiente Episcopo et ipso Episcopo praesente aut eius delegato, statutis temporibus congregentur . . . Ad Episcopum loci spectat inter diaconos in dioecesi operantes spiritum communionis alere, evitando ne ille 'corporativismus' efformetur, qui praeteritis saeculis tantopere ad diaconatum permanentem evanescendum influxit."

276. "Specifica vocatio diaconi permanentis stabilitatem in hoc ordine supponit. Fortuitus igitur transitus ad presbyteratum diaconorum permanentium, non uxoratorum vel viduorum, rarissima exceptio semper erit, quae admitti non poterit, nisi graves et speciales rationes id suadeant." *Directorium* no. 5.

277. LG 29a gives a reference to *Constitutiones Ecclesiae Aegypciacae,* III, 2: ed. Funk, *Didascalia* II, 103; *Statuta Eccl. ant.* 37–41: Mansi 3, 954 (but in fact it is taken from *Statuta Eccl. ant.* 4: Mansi 3, 951). The text of the *Statuta* 92 (4), CChr SL 148, 181, says: "Diaconus cum ordinatur, solus episcopus, qui eum benedicit, manum super caput illius ponat, quia non ad sacerdotium sed ad ministerium consecratur."

278. Cf. *Pontifical Romano-Germanique* (950), vol. 1, Città del Vaticano 1963, 24. In the present *Pontificale Romanum* (Ed. Typ. 1968, 1989), the following expressions are found: "The mission of the deacon is a help for the bishop and his priests (episcopo eiusque presbyterio adiumentum) in the service of the word, of the altar, and of charity" (opening address by the bishop); the deacon is ordained "in the service of the Church (ad ministerium Ecclesiae)" and "to provide help to the order of priests (in adiutorium ordinis sacerdotalis)" (bishop's questions to the ordinands). In the consecratory prayer it is recalled that the apostles "chose seven men to help them in daily service." It will be noted that in the case of a priest, the question asked is whether he "wishes to become a priest, collaborator with the bishops in the priesthood, to serve and guide the people of God under the guidance of the Holy Spirit."

279. The Latin version (L) says: "In diacono ordinando solus episcopus imponat manus, propterea quia non in sacerdotio ordinatur, sed in ministerio episcopi, ut faciat ea quae ab ipso iubentur." *Trad. apost.* (ed. B. Botte), SCh 11(2), Paris 1968, 58.

280. The interpretation given by the Council Commission is also controversial: "Verba desumuntur ex Statutis Eccl. Ant. . . . et significant diaconos non ad corpus et sanguinem Domini offerendum, sed ad servitium caritatis in Ecclesia ordinari," AS III/8, 101.

281. "Et utique sacramentum nemo potest conficere, nisi sacerdos, qui rite fuerit ordinatus . . ." Conc. Lateran IV (1215), DS 802; cf. *Trad. Apost.*, 4.

282. "Forma sacerdotii talis est: 'Accipe potestatem offerendi sacrificium in Ecclesia pro vivis et mortuis . . .'" Conc. Florence (1439), DS 1326.

283. Conc. Trent (1563), DS 1771; cf. likewise DS 1764: ." . . Apostolis eorumque successoribus in sacerdotio potestatem traditam consecrandi, offerendi et ministrandi corpus et sanguinem eius, nec non et peccata dimittendi et retinendi . . ."

284. ." . . distinctio ordinis est accipienda secundum relationem ad Eucharistiam. Quia potestas ordinis aut est ad consecrationem Eucharistiae ipsius, aut ad aliquod ministerium ordinandum ad hoc. Si primo modo, sic est ordo sacerdotum. Et ideo, cum ordinantur, accipiunt calicem cum vino et patenam cum pane, potestatem accipientes consecrandi corpus et sanguinem Christi." Saint Thomas, *STh* III, *Suppl.* q37 a2 resp..

285. ." . . episcopatus non est ordo, secundum quod ordo est quoddam sacramentum . . . ordinatur omnis ordo ad eucharistiae sacramentum; unde, cum Episcopus non habeat potestatem superiorem sacerdote quantum ad hoc, non erit episcopatus ordo." Saint Thomas, *In IV Sent.* d24 q3, a2, sol. II.

286. LG 11a. The statement of the central value of the Eucharist is repeated several times. Cf. PO 5b ("in Sanctissima . . . Eucharistia totum bonum spirituale Ecclesiae continetur"), UR 15a ("celebrationem eucharisticam, fontem vitae ecclesiae et pignus futurae gloriae"), CD 30f ("ut celebratio Eucharistici Sacrificii centrum sit et culmen totius vitae communitatis christianae").

287. "Sacerdos quidem ministerialis, potestate sacra qua gaudet, populum sacerdotalem efformat ac regit, sacrificium eucharisticum in persona Christi conficit illudque nomine totius populi Dei offert . . ." LG 10b.

288. Cf. SC 35d ("authorized person," which also includes deacons), LG 20c (adiutoribus . . . diaconis), LG 28a(ministerium ecclesiasticum . . . diaconi), LG 29a (ad ministerium), LG 41d (ministri, imprimis diaconi), OE 17 (institutum diaconatus), CD 15a (diaconi, qui ad ministerium ordinati), DV 25a (clericos omnes . . . qui ut diaconi), AG 15i (munera . . . diaconorum), AG 16f (salutis ministros in ordine . . . diaconorum . . . ordo diaconatus).

289. "Doctrina catholica, in liturgia, Magisterio et constanti Ecclesiae explicita praxi, agnoscit duos gradus participationis ministerialis exsistere sacerdotii Christi: Episcopatum et presbyteratum. Diaconatus ad illos adiuvandos atque ad illis serviendum destinatur. Propterea verbum *sacerdos* designat, in usu hodierno, Episcopos et presbyteros, sed non diaconos. Tamen doctrina catholica docet gradus participationis sacerdotalis (Episcopatum et presbyteratum) et gradum servitii (diaconatum) conferri, hos omnes tres, actu sacramentali qui 'ordinatio' appellatur, id est, sacramento Ordinis," CCE no. 1554. La *Ratio Fundamentalis* nos. 4 and 5, also avoids applying terms of "priesthood" etc. to deacons: ." . . ad eius (cuiusque ministri ordinati) plenam veritatem pertinet esse participatio specifica et repraesentatio ministerii Christi... manuum impositio diaconum non est 'ad sacerdotium sed ad ministerium,' id est non ad celebrationem eucharisticam sed ad servitium . . . is (diaconus) enim, prout unici ministerii ecclesiastici particeps, est in Ecclesia specificum signum sacramentale Christi servi."

290. "Sacerdotium autem commune fidelium et sacerdotium ministeriale seu hierarchicum, licet essentia et non gradu tantum differant, ad invicem tamen ordinantur; unum enim et alterum suo peculiari modo de uno Christi sacerdotio participant." LG 10b.

291. "Missionis autem et gratiae supremi Sacerdotis peculiari modo participes sunt inferioris quoque ordinis ministri, imprimis Diaconi . . ." LG 41d. Referring to this text, CCE no. 1570 replaces the expression "supreme Sacerdotis" by that of "Christi": "Diaconi missionem et gratiam Christi, modo speciali participant."

292. "Sacramento ordinis ex divina institutione inter christifideles quidam charactere indelebili quo signantur, constituuntur sacri ministri, qui nempe consecrantur et deputantur ut, pro suo quisque gradu, in persona Christi Capitis munera docendi, sanctificandi et regendi adimplentes, Dei populum pascant," can. 1008. "Ordines sunt episcopatus, presbyteratus et diaconatus," can. 1009. The 1983 CIC uses the expression "sacri ministri" to designate the baptized faithful who have received sacramental ordination. On one hand its expressions are briefer than those of Vatican II, and do not quote LG 29; on the other, despite the qualification "pro suo gradu," it goes further than the explicit texts of Vatican II in applying the notion of "in persona Christi Capitis" to the diaconate.

293. Cf. the data given in Chapter VI.

294. Cf., e.g., Tertullian, *De exh. cast.* 7, 5 (CCh SL 319, 94), in which bishops, priests and deacons constitute the "ordo sacerdotalis" or "sacerdotium"; Leo I, Ep. 12,5; 14,3f. (PL 54, 652, 672f.), who also adds subdeacons as members of the "ordo sacerdotalis"; Optatus of Milevis, *Contra Parmen.* I, 13 (SCh 412, 200), for whom deacons formed part of the "third priesthood" ("Quid diaconos in tertio, quid presbyteros in secundo sacerdotio constitutos?"); also Saint Jerome, *Ep.* 48, 21 (CSEL 54, 387): "Episcopi, presbyteri, diaconi aut virgines eliguntur aut vidui aut certe post sacerdotium in aeternum pudici."

295. Cf. Conc. Trent, DS 1764.

296. Cf. note 279 *supra.*

297. CCE no. 1569 itself, citing the formula of the *Traditio* and LG 29, underlines the fact that the bishop alone imposes his hands on the deacon at ordination, as a sign of a special connection with him: "Pro diacono ordinando, solus Episcopus manus imponit, ita significans diaconum in muneribus suae 'diaconiae' Episcopo speciatim annecti."

298. ." . . episcopos, qui munus ministerii sui vario gradu, variis subiectis in ecclesia legitime tradiderunt," LG 28.

299. "Gratia enim sacramentali roborati, in diaconia liturgiae, verbi et caritatis populo Dei, in communione cum episcopo eiusque presbyterio, inserviunt," LG 29. The *Directorium* (no. 22) speaks of assistance given to "bishops" and "priests": "Sic diaconus auxiliatur et inservit episcopis et presbyteris, qui semper praesunt liturgiae, praevigilant super doctrinam et moderantur Populum Dei."

300. "In this ancient text the 'ministry' is described as 'service of the bishop'; the Council lays the stress on service to the People of God." *Insegnamenti* XVI/II 1000.

301. "Inter varia illa ministeria quae inde a primis temporibus in Ecclesia exercentur, teste traditione, praecipuum locum tenet munus illorum qui, in episcopatum constituti, per successionem ab initio recurrentem, apostolici seminis traduces habent . . . Proinde docet Sacra Synodus Episcopos ex divina institutione in locum Apostolorum successisse, tamquam Ecclesiae pastores . . ." LG 20; "Episcopi, utpote apostolorum successores, a Domino . . .

missionem accipiunt . . ." LG 24a. In the same sense, cf. DS 1768, 3061, CCE no. 1555.

302. "Christus, quem Pater sanctificavit et misit in mundum (John 10:36), consecrationis missionisque suae per apostolos suos, eorum successores, videlicet Episcopos participes effecit, qui munus ministerii sui, vario gradu, variis subiectis in Ecclesia legitime tradiderunt. Sic ministerium ecclesiasticum divinitus institutum diversis ordinibus exercetur ab illis qui iam ab antiquo Episcopi, Presbyteri, Diaconi vocantur." LG 28a.

303. "Ordo est sacramentum per quod missio a Christo Ipsius Apostolis concredita exerceri pergit in Ecclesia usque ad finem temporum: est igitur ministerii apostolici sacramentum. Tres implicat gradus: Episcopatum, presbyteratum et diaconatum." CCE no. 1536.

304. See, even, the expression "ministerial or hierarchical priesthood" in LG 10b.

305. "Apostolis eorumque successoribus a Christo collatum est munus in ipsius nomine et potestate docendi, sanctificandi et regendi," AA 2b; cf. LG 19a.

306. "Munus autem illud, quod Dominus pastoribus populi sui commisit, verum est cervitium quod in sacris Litteris *diakonia* seu ministerium significanter nuncupatur," LG 24a.

307. Cf. Conc. Trent, DS 1764 (". . . Apostolis eorumque successoribus in sacerdotio potestatem traditam consecrandi . . ."), DS 1771 (". . . sacerdotium visibile et externum . . ."), DS 1765 (". . . tam sancti sacerdotii ministerium . . . ministrorum ordines, qui sacerdotio ex officio deservirent . . ."), DS 1772 (". . . alios ordines, et maiores et minores, per quos velut per gradus quosdam in sacerdotium tendatur . . .").

308. Cf. LG 29a.

309. E.g., Mgr. Yü Pin thought that permanent deacons could exercise a function "pontis seu mediationis inter hierarchiam et christifideles," AS II/II, 431; likewise the Conciliar Commission retained the idea that married deacons could constitute "quasi pontem" between the clergy and the people, AS III/1, 267.

310. "Concilium denique Vaticanum II optatis et precibus suffragatum est, ut Diaconatus permanens, ubi id animarum bono conduceret, instauretur veluti medius ordo inter superiores ecclesiasticae hierarchiae gradus et reliquum populum Dei, quasi interpres necessitatum ac votorum christianorum communitatum, instimulator famulatus seu *diaconiae* Ecclesiae apud locales christianas communitates, signum vel sacramentum ipsius Christi Domini, qui non venit ministrari, sed ministrare." Paul VI, *Ad Pascendum,* AAS 54 (1972) 536.

311. "Per receptum diaconatum aliquis fit clericus et incardinatur Ecclesiae particulari vel Praelaturae personali pro cuius servitio promotus est," CIC can. 266; cf. also cann. 1008–9, which are echoed in the 1998 *Directorium,* no. 1: "Per impositionem manuum et consecrationis precem ipse minister sacer et hierarchiae membrum constituitur. Haec conditio ipsius statum theologicum et iuridicum in Ecclesia determinat."

312. Cf. *Trad. apost.* 4, 8, 21, 24 (bridging function between the bishop and the Christian people); *STh* III q82 a3 ad1 ("diaconi sunt inter sacerdotes et populum").

313. Thus they can be married (can. 281, 3), they are not obliged to wear ecclesiastical dress (can. 284), or to abstain from holding public office in the civil sphere (can. 285, 3) or from administering property; they can devote themselves to business and commerce (can. 286) and take an active part in party politics and trades unions (can. 287, 2; cf. can. 288). In this regard, see the further clarifications made in the *Directorium,* nos. 7–14.

314. E.g.: the capacity to exercise power of government or jurisdiction by reason of one's order (can. 129); to obtain posts whose exercise requires the power of order or government (can. 274, 1) although they cannot be vicars-general or bishops (can. 475); deacons can be appointed diocesan judges (can. 1421, 1) and even the only judge (can. 1425, 4); they can also confer certain dispensations (can. 89; can. 1079, 2), or, as a general faculty, assist at weddings (can. 1111f.); they are ordinary ministers of Baptism (can. 861, 1), of Communion (can. 910, 1) and of the exposition of the Eucharist (can. 943); they can preach everywhere (can. 764) and the homily is reserved to them as it is to the priests (can. 767, 1).

315. Cf. *Zukunft aus der Kraft des Konzils. Die ausserordentliche Bischofssynode 1985. Die Dokumente mit einem Kommentar von W. Kasper,* Freiburg 1986; W. Kasper, *Kirche als Communio,* in: Id., *Theologie und Kirche,* Mainz 1987, 272–289.

316. "in diaconia liturgiae, verbi et caritatis Populo Dei . . . inserviunt . . . fidelium cultui et orationi praesidere . . . caritatis et administrationis officiis dediti . . ." LG 29a. The Conciliar Commission clarified it in these terms: "Indicantur officia diaconorum in primis modo generali, brevi sed gravi sententia, in triplici campo, scilicet 'in diaconia liturgiae, verbi et caritatis': quod deinde magis specificatur per 'caritatis et administrationis officia'," AS III/1, 260. The stress laid on the charitable dimension is also evident in the explanation given by the same Commission with regard to the formula "non ad sacerdotium, sed ad ministerium": "significant diaconos non ad corpus et sanguinem Domini offerentes, sed ad servitium caritatis in Ecclesia ordinari," AS III/8, 101.

317. "Iuvat enim viros, qui ministerio vere diaconali fungantur, vel verbum divinum tamquam catechistae praedicantes, vel nomine parochi et episcopi dissitas communitates christianas moderantes, vel caritatem exercentes in operibus socialibus seu caritativis, per impositionem manuum inde ab Apostolis traditam corroborari et altari arctius coniungi, ut ministerium suum per gratiam sacramentalem diaconatus efficacius expleant." AG 16f.

318. "ubi sacerdos deest, Ecclesiae nomine matrimoniis celebrandis assistere et benedicere ex delegatione episcopi vel parochi . . . funeris ac sepulturae ritibus praeesse . . . praesidere, ubi sacerdos non adest . . . caritatis et administrationis officiis atque socialis subsidii operibus, Hierarchiae nomine, perfungi . . . apostolica laicorum opera fovere et adiuvare," *Sacrum diaconatus* no. 22 (AAS 59, 1967, 701f.).

319. On the tasks appointed to them and the questions raised by can. 517, 2, cf. *supra* cap. IV notes 162–163.

320. When it speaks of deacons, it says quite simply: "Ad diaconos pertinet, inter alia, Episcopo et presbyteris in mysteriorum divinorum celebratione assistere, maxime Eucharistiae, eamque distribuere, Matrimonio assistere idque benedicere, Evangelium proclamare et praedicare, exsequiis praesidere atque se diversis caritatis consecrare servitiis," CCE no. 1570. When it makes an explicit reference to the permanent diaconate, citing AG 16, it reaffirms that it is appropriate and useful to give sacramental ordination to "viros qui in Ecclesia ministerium vere diaconale explent sive in vita liturgica et pastorali sive in operibus socialibus et caritativis," CCE no. 1571.

321. "Ad munus docendi . . . quidem elucet ex libri Evangelii traditione, in ipso ordinationis ritu praescripta. Diaconi munus sanctificandi impletur . . . quo pacto apparet quomodo ministerium diaconale ex Eucharistia procedat ad eandemque redeat, nec in mero servitio sociali exhauriri possit. Munus regendi denique exercetur per deditionem operibus caritatis . . . peculiari habito ad caritatem, quae praeeminentem diaconalis ministerii notam constituit." *Ratio* no. 9.

322. "Diaconi proprium officium est Evangelium proclamare et Verbum Dei praedicare . . . quae facultas oritur e sacramento . . . Ministerio Episcopi et, subordinate, ministerio presbyterorum, diaconus praestat auxilium sacramentale, ac proinde intrinsecum, organicum, a confusione alienum . . . Opera caritatis, dioecesana vel paroecialia, quae sunt inter primaria officia Episcopi et presbyterorum, ab his transmittuntur, secundum testimonium Traditionis Ecclesiae, servis ministerii ecclesiastici, hoc est diaconis . . ." *Directorium*, nos. 24, 28, 37.

323. E.g.: "Itaque Diaconatus in Ecclesia mirabiliter effloruit simulque insigne praebuit testimonium amoris erga Christum ac fratres in caritatis

operibus exsequendis, in ritibus sacris celebrandis atque in pastoralibus perfungendis muneribus." Paul VI, *Ad Pascendum,* AAS 64 (1972) 535.

324. Cf. notes 249, 281, 282 *supra.*

325. Cf. note 283 *supra.*

326. LG 21b notes succinctly: "Episcoporum est per Sacramentum Ordinis novos electos in corpus episcopale assumere."

327. E.g.: "Minister ordinarius sacrae communionis est Episcopus, presbyter et diaconus. Extraordinarius sacrae communionis minister est acolythus necnon alius christifidelis ad normam can. 230, 3 deputatus." CIC can. 910.

328. "Confirmationis minister ordinarius est Episcopus; valide hoc sacramentum confert presbyter quoque hac facultate vi iuris communis aut peculiaris concessionis competentis auctoritatis instructus." CIC can. 882.

329. LG 26c considers bishops to be "dispensatores sacrorum ordinum," while CIC can. 1012 states that "sacrae ordinationis minister est Episcopus consecratus"; cf. likewise DS 1326 and 1777. Nevertheless, the problem raised by some papal documents that seemed to grant a priest the faculty of conferring the diaconate (cf. DS 1435) and even the priesthood (cf. DS 1145, 1146, 1290) does not appear to have been settled doctrinally.

330. The *Ratio Fundamentalis* itself (no. 9) says this: "Ministerium diaconale distinctum est exercitio trium munerum, ministerio ordinato propriorum, in specifica luce diaconiae."

331. Constitutio apostolica *Sacramentum ordinis,* art. 4–5 (DS 3857–3861). On the imposition of hands and the prayer of consecration, cf. also Gregory IX, Ep. *Presbyter et diaconus* ad episc. Olaf de Lund (DS 826; cf. 1326).

332. *Ministeria quaedam,* in: AAS 64 (1972) 531.

333. *Sacrum diaconatus,* in: AAS 59 (1967) 698.

334. The International Theological Commission has been notified that a revised version of this canon is in preparation, aiming to distinguish the priestly ("sacerdotal") ministries from the diaconal ministry.

335. Cf. Erdö, *Der ständige Diakon. Theologisch-systematische und rechtliche Erwägungen,* in: AkathKR 166 (1997) 79–80.

336. *Ad Trall.* 3, 1; SCh 10(2), 96.

Msgr. Reynold Hillenbrand
1904-1979

Monsignor Reynold Hillenbrand, ordained a priest by Cardinal George Mundelein in 1929, was Rector of St. Mary of the Lake Seminary from 1936 to 1944.

He was a leading figure in the liturgical and social action movement in the United States during the 1930s and worked to promote active, intelligent, and informed participation in the Church's liturgy.

He believed that a reconstruction of society would occur as a result of the renewal of the Christian spirit, whose source and center is the liturgy.

Hillenbrand taught that, since the ultimate purpose of Catholic action is to Christianize society, the renewal of the liturgy must undoubtedly play the key role in achieving this goal.

Hillenbrand Books strives to reflect the spirit of Monsignor Reynold Hillenbrand's pioneering work by making available innovative and scholarly resources that advance the liturgical and sacramental life of the Church.